Walkin' the Walk
While Talkin' the Law

In memory of
Jonathon "Skip" Chase

by Stephen Foehr
with George "Ron" Waldie

Copyright © 2011 by Stephen Foehr & George Ron Waldie
All rights reserved.

"Jazzer," "Taffeta" and "In Rural Vermont" Copyright © 2011 Linda Chase. Used by permission. "Skip Chase" Copyright © 2011 Len Rose-Avila. Used by permission. "The Delta" reprinted by permission of Colorado Law Review.

The use of any part of this publication reproduced, transmitted in any form or by any means, electronic, mechanical, photocopying, recording or otherwise, or stored in a retrieval system without the prior written consent of the authors or, in case of photocopying or other reprographic copying, a license from the United States Licensing Agency is an infringement of the copyright law.

Foehr, Stephen
Waldie, George Ron with an introduction by George Waldie.
Includes Bibliographical references.

Published in 2011 by George Ron Waldie, Boulder, Colo.
All rights reserved. No part of the contents of this book may be reproduced without the written permission of the authors.

Printed and bound in the United States of America

For Nancy, Adam, Tamara, Rebecca, and Eli.

In loving memory of Linda Chase, Skip's sister, who contributed greatly to the content of this book.

In memory of Dan Israel who was one, if not the best, friend of Skip.

And, in memory of Dean David Getches, a close friend to the Chase family, without whose support this book would not have happened.

I have waited too long to write this book; so many of those who have contributed are leaving us.

Finally, this book is dedicated to all those bright, legal minds, both now and in the future, who choose to practice public interest and/or poverty law.

Contents

Chapter 1	Action Justice	13
Chapter 2	The Private Man	22
Chapter 3	A Hoe, a File and a Clorox Bottle	38
Chapter 4	Bringing Law to the Fields	67
Chapter 5	San Luis Valley	81
Chapter 6	Them vs. Us	93
Chapter 7	CRLS v. SEC. OF AGRICULTURE	100
Chapter 8	Enemies Attack CRLS	106
Chapter 9	Coup Against Skip	111
Chapter 10	Life after CRLS	118
Chapter 11	Skip, Dean of Vermont Law School	132
Appendix A	Summary of Proposals	156
Appendix B	Cases Litigated by Jonathon B. Chase	159
Appendix C	Publications by Jonathon B. Chase	167
Contributors		169
Bibliography		171
Index		174

Jazzer

*My brother can dance
to jazz and rock and roll
though he trained through
foxtrot, rumba and waltz
which is not true of every
dead man you can think of.
Mostly the others lie around
or visit old friends on earth
without evoking anything.
No sneaking up in the dark—
they just appear in a hazy
outline at the end of
long carpeted corridors.
My brother (like our Pop)
drops in on a drum roll
and a cymbal crash,
a trumpet blast, tenor sax—
he's just so fucking
finger-snapping cool.
Nothing creepy about him.
He brings his friends
along on vinyl—The MJQ,
Miles, Brubeck and Coltrane.
Every time I think of him
he's at a Newport party
and never forgets to put me
on the guest list*

—Linda Chase

Preface

My association with Jonathon "Skip" Chase, when we were both working with farm workers, motivated me to write this book. He was working with Colorado Rural Legal Services (CRLS), which he co-founded with Bill Prakken; I was working with the Colorado Migrant Council (CMC). Both programs were funded by the Office of Economic Opportunity (OEO), made available in 1964 by President Lyndon Johnson's War on Poverty and run by Sargent Shriver. Our efforts were targeted at migrant and seasonal farm workers. My first introduction to Skip was in Delta, Colorado, where he was posing as a farm worker. That caught my eye.

My admiration for Skip grew from those incredible attorneys he hired to litigate cases for poor people dealing with divorce, physical abuse, rent and wage issues, simple traffic violations and, most importantly, housing and health issues. Poor people in rural Colorado, in general, had no access to legal representation until CRLS came along; then we (CMC) were able to address those issues in ways we had not been able to do before.

We at CMC became the outreach and community organizers that fed cases to CRLS. Both programs worked well together. The efforts of both organizations forced state and federal agencies, responsible for migrant farm workers, to be more conscientious and legally responsible in performing their duties concerning labor, housing and health conditions.

Both Skip and I got caught up in the Mexican and Native American cultures and the needs of these people to have legal, educational and health rights addressed. He did that in a noble way. He was fearless in his approach, which was needed to deal with these issues. Skip's philosophy of providing legal representation to ALL was instilled and carried out by those capable attorneys that he hired. I am not sure that any of this would have happened with anyone else—anyone who did not possess his personality and drive.

I was also motivated to write this book when I visited the University of Colorado (CU) Law School, where I looked around for something honoring Jonathon "Skip" Chase and the Colorado Rural Legal Services program. Finding nothing, I made my way to then Dean David Getches' office and told him my thoughts. David surprised me by saying that he agreed and wanted new faculty and students to know who Skip was and what he and the others accomplished. As a result, a plaque honoring Skip and the students who receive his fellowship now hangs in the Law Clinic study room.

While visiting the CU Law School, I interrupted a group of about twleve students and asked them if they knew the name Skip Chase. All shook their heads "no". One asked me to give them a hint. When I explained that he was a former law professor at CU and co-founder of CRLS, their eyebrows shot up, indicating they were familiar with that program. I decided then to provide Skip's life story for both the CU Law School and the Vermont Law School, where he served as Dean.

I hope that law students in pursuit of careers in public interest or poverty law will find this book inspirational. Many of the young lawyers of CRLS have gone on to successful careers, as both attorneys and judges, including appellate and state supreme court appointments. To Norm Aaronson, Jean and Frank Dubofsky, and Don Miller, you have my appreciation for your contributions as they guided me to others who were an important part of that time period. In particular, I want to thank my friend, Michael Evans Smith, who has for many years attempted to document this important part of American history. This book, I hope, is a beginning, and he, Magdaleno Avila, and others can finish this story. It was an honor for me to have met all of the contributors and to produce this book.

For Nancy, Skip's widow, I hope we did this right and that you will appreciate the story of which you were such a big part.

—George Ron Waldie

Chapter 1

Action Justice

When their six-month-old baby came down with pneumonia, the distraught parents took the child to the Conejos County Hospital in La Jara, Colorado. Two days later, the hospital refused to release the baby without guaranteed payment of the $130 bill. The mother and father, migrant farm workers putting in 10-hour days working the potato fields for minimum wages, didn't have the cash.

Their child was being held for "baby mortgage" until they could make good on the bill owed.

Too poor to hire a lawyer, speaking little English, clueless how to negotiate with a seemingly uncaring system, the young mother and father felt helpless. Like thousands of other migrant farm workers toiling in Colorado fields, they were denied Medicare.

Jonathon 'Skip' Chase had people like these despairing parents in mind when he co-founded the Colorado Rural Legal Service (CRLS) in 1969 with Bill Prakken. A University of Colorado law associate professor at the time, Skip was passionate that law be in the service of everyone regardless of economic or social status, ethnicity or religion. Lawyers had the duty to fight for the right of disadvantage persons to have access to the courts and legal counsel. This principle, basic to American democracy, took Professor Chase out of the classroom and into the fields with migrant workers.

"Equal justice under law," inscribed in stone over the entrance to the United States Supreme Court building, served as Skip's mantra.

At the age of six, at summer camp, Jonathon chose the name Skip for himself. His younger sister, who attended the camp with him, remembered the choice might have been related to Skippy peanut butter. As he grew into adulthood, Skip never lost his natural boyhood characteristics: the twinkle in the eye that said life should be fun; the sincere personal touch that made people genuinely feel he cared for them; the enthusiasm to put his thumb in as many of life's pies as possible.

A barely discernable line distinguished the personal from the professional Skip: both wore, at times, hair long and a beard, sported beads of coral or turquoise, favored blue jeans and work shirts, loved to play the bongos and perform in skits. Only when Skip appeared in court to argue a case did the professional subsume the personal. Then, he wore an appropriate dark business suit, white shirt and conservative tie. He spoke as a well-prepared, erudite and very smart lawyer— although the glint in his eye didn't disappear.

His personal commitment to the legal principle of equal justice inspired a corps of young talented attorneys to join him in the fight. Many of those idealistic attorneys, the core of CRLS, became judges and continue to uphold the spirit of equal justice; all the while Skip worked in academia, eventually to become Dean of the Vermont Law School.

In the "baby mortgage" case, CRLS attorneys accompanied the parents to meet with the hospital's officials. The CRLS lawyers, sitting at a conference table with the parents, hospital administrator Wayne M. Miller and financial officer Louis Mott, stated their case: the hospital, having received federal funds under the Public Health Service Act, popularly known as Hill-Burton Act, was required by law to provide a reasonable volume of free or low-cost medical care to needy individuals. That was one of the conditions of receiving the federal money. The other requirements set by Congress were that construction or expansion of a hospital be consistent with the state plan for having reasonable allocation of medical care facilities around the state and no discrimination based on race or ethnicity.

The hospital officers insisted they had a fiscal responsibility for the hospital's financial wellbeing and refused to release the baby until the parents signed a promissory note for $130.

After hours of back-and-forth, an agreement was reached; the parents got their baby back immediately and the hospital eventually received payment.

This wasn't the only case where CRLS attorneys fought for health care rights of their indigent clients. When northern Colorado Weld County General Hospital, which had received $1.6 million in federal money under the Hill-Burton Act, balked at providing a reasonable amount of free or low-income medical care to the poor, CRLS attorneys Jon Asher and Jean Dubofsky, under the guidance and support of Skip, brought suit.

Weld County Commissioner Glen Billings stated the CRLS action was a "harassment suit only."

CRLS responded that "poor people are asserting their legal rights in courts for the first time in this nation's history, and people who had not previously been held accountable to poor people through the courts are now being held accountable. Until such persons become accustomed to the right of poor persons to exercise their legal rights through lawsuits, such suits will be characterized as frivolous."

The Weld County General Hospital suit was a nationally important case, according to Asher, who later became the Executive Director of the Colorado Legal Services (CLS), "The case led to access to hospital care for low-income people throughout the country. Such people derived huge benefits."

The suit was brought on behalf of Rafaela Euresti, a pregnant migrant worker who sought prenatal care. "Our suit was different than the La Jara hospital case in that the La Jara case was not based in broad federal law," Asher said, sitting at a conference table in the downtown Denver CLS office. "It was more a collection practice rather than providing care. In my opinion, the case was about outrageous behavior. I think it was enslavement, kidnapping."

Asher wore a dark blue blazer and grey slacks, a look as conservative as his approach to law, which he admitted is more prudent than Skip's method. Beneath his calm demeanor, he brims with the same ardent passion that fueled Skip's mission in law. He has devoted his professional life to the aid and defense of people who cannot afford legal services.

"At the time, Weld General Hospital required pregnant migrant women either to provide proof of insurance or to put up a $500 cash bond to pay for the delivery," Asher said. "Of course, migrant workers neither had health insurance or $500. The hospital didn't want to treat such people. They wanted them to make their way to Colorado General in Denver. Some of the women did and some made it half way before delivering. Others waited in the Weld General parking lot. The hospital wouldn't let them give birth on its doorstep. As soon as the woman in the parking lot gave birth, the hospital would ship her off to Colorado General."

Asher and Dubofsky lost the case in the U.S. District Court. The court ruled that the Hill-Burton Act "did not create any contractual relationship between the United States and appellees; that, if it did, appellants have no standing to sue; and that, in any event, the action was barred by the Act itself in 42 U.S.C. Sec. 291m,2 limiting federal supervision or control of hospital administration."

The CRLS attorneys appealed to United States Court of Appeals, Tenth District, which reversed the District Court ruling (cite as: 458 F.2d 1115). "There is no doubt by adopting this portion of the Hill-Burton Act, Congress intended to benefit indigents in the position of the appellants," wrote Justice Clark. "Congress expressed its purpose in the Act as 'to assist the several states in the carrying out of their programs…to furnish adequate hospital, clinic, or similar services to all their people…'"

Such cases were fought and won because Skip Chase walked the line between legal reasoning and spontaneously jumping to the aid of people being treated unfairly. He believed that injustices must be challenged and acted on that principle in his professional and private life.

He once broke into a jail to consult with a client. The incident happened in Crested Butte, Colorado, a small mountain town best known for skiing. During the winter season, the town of 1,550 is jammed to the rafters with skiers. But in the summer, the burg falls back into being a sleepy charming historic mining town. CRLS held a staff meeting in Crested Butte because the location in southwest Colorado was near CRLS major programs and accommodations were readily available in the low-tourist season.

After the meeting, the CRLS attorneys held a party at John Kuenhold's house. During the hilarities, the dog of Stan Wagner, one of the attorneys, escaped. Wagner drove around town calling "Free Huey! Free Huey!" The dog was named after Huey Newton, a founding member of the Black Panthers jailed for what many perceived as political activism. At one point, he stopped in front of the fire station across from Kuenhold's house. The town constable confronted

Wagner, who had a notoriously short temper, about blocking the fire station's entrance.

"Stan and the cop got into it," recalled Bill Prakken, who was on the scene, "and Stan was arrested and taken to jail." Hearing that Wagner had been incarcerated, Skip rushed to his rescue with the troop of fellow lawyers at his heels. "Our cry was, 'Huey Newton is free but Stan's in jail'," Prakken laughed.

The jail's front door was locked. Skip knocked. From the other side the sheriff asked what he wanted. Skip introduced himself in a reasonable lawyerly way and asked to consult with his client. The sheriff refused to open the door or admit Skip. Banging on the door, Skip demanded he be allowed to meet with his client. Again the sheriff refused from behind the locked door.

Injustice demands direct action; that was Skip's credo. Balling his fist, he broke the door's glass pane, reached in and calmly unlocked the door. When he stepped into the jail, followed by the pushing crowd of CRLS attorneys, the incensed sheriff promptly arrested him and several of the attorneys.

Mob is too strong a description although the lawyers waved their arms and hurled mob-like demands at the outnumbered sheriff. Feeling under siege, the law officer called the state highway patrol for reinforcements to, in the words of one CRLS attorney present, "quell a potential riot of lawyers."

Skip gained access to his client and secured his release.

"In CRLS lore, that's called the Crested Butte Massacre," Prakken chuckled at the memory.

This acute sense of justice and spur-of-the-moment willingness to fight for an individual's rights was integral in how Skip conducted his life. Even the seemingly mundane task of getting a Sunbeam mix-master repaired became a crusade for due process and consumer rights. When the family's mix-master failed because of faulty wiring, Skip took the machine back to the store to have it fixed—and got in a legal battle.

Here's how Skip told the story:

"I was informed (by the store manager) that our Sunbeam would be repaired but that I would have to pay transportation charges to have it sent to and from Denver, where the work would be done," he wrote in an account of the incident. *"The amount I was to pay was, as I recall, somewhere around five dollars. I, of course, refused to pay, asserting my right to have this defective piece of merchandise fixed without any cost to me whatever."*

The injustice of the big guy (the corporation) sticking the small guy (the consumer) with an unfair burden and, salt in the wound, in violation of the Uniform Commercial Code raised Skip's hackles.

"He (store manager) responded by telling me that he had no duty to fix the machine since their store had not manufactured it and that they were merely agreeing to have it fixed as a customer courtesy for transportation costs. I immediately cited section 2-314 of the Uniform Commercial Code and told him that, as a seller, he was indeed responsible for the perfection of the Sunbeam mix-master.

"That did him in. He immediately demanded to know where I was from, a subtle recognition of the fact that my oral delivery and physical stature did not mark me as a cowboy from Durango. I had been identified as someone undoubtedly from New York and, to the more sophisticated, perhaps even a Jew. (This inquiry relating to my land of origin is not one unlike that I received from an irate Vermonter who objected to my using up valuable road space with my bicycle and accused me of being from, of all things, New Jersey.) When I refused to answer his question, indicating that I did not quite see the relevance

of it, he stood firm in his insistence that my Sunbeam would not be fixed without the transportation money."

Then the standoff, a familiar stance Skip often took in his professional life. He drew himself up to his full five feet eight inches and declared,

"I therefore am forced to revoke my acceptance and am returning this machine."

To which the manager responded, "Say what?"

"He was apparently not familiar with the requirements of section 2-608 of the Uniform Commercial Code. I sought to enlighten him by explaining that the law gave me the right to return this defective machine and to have my money returned."

To which the manager retorted, "Fat chance."

Skip left the defective mix-master sitting on the store's counter. Later in the week he called and spoke with the owner.

"He told me that, although they certainly did not have to, they had acquiesced in my altogether unreasonable demand and would repair the Sunbeam entirely at their expense, including transportation, however, by telling me that because of my bad attitude I was no longer welcome at his hardware store.

"What I realized over the years in Colorado was that the prevailing ethic there demanded consumer subservience. Complainers were immediately branded as troublemakers and malcontents.... The global point of all this is one I have made before but from a somewhat different perspective. The early complainers are those who really begin the educational process. It is those people who are ahead of

their times and who enlighten the rest of us. It is they who dare to think the unthinkable...."

In Colorado, Skip identified with the migrant workers and the rural poor "complainers" not served by a legal service. He set out to discover their plight first hand and then create a remedy.

Chapter 2

The Private Man

Jonathon Boyd Chase, born in 1939 to Lillian and David Boyd Chase, grew up in a "fairly wealthy home with a live-in maid," according to his eldest son Adam, a tax attorney. Skip's hometown Manhasset, on Long Island's North Shore, was an upper middle-class enclave of large yards and bosky streets, a quiet safe place to raise a family. Upscale stores like B Altman's and Lord & Taylor reflected the taste and style of the residents. Now, stores like Prada, Giogrio Armani, Louis Vuitton and Hermes anchor the town's high-end premium "Miracle Mile" shopping center.

The Chase family, mom, dad, Skip and younger sister Linda, lived in the new development Strathmore, a step up from the Jewish ghetto in Newark where Lillian and David had started. By the time Skip and Linda reached high school, the family relocated to a large house in Flower Hill, where they had a backyard swimming pool and live peacocks decorating the lawn.

"There were golf clubs, country clubs, yacht clubs and wonderful schools," Linda said. "But there was also the residue of imbedded prejudice. My parents had to wait a long time to find a golf club that would accept them. Our family was still considered by the WASPs to be Jewish and, although this was never talked about at home, Skip and I gradually realized that we were considered to be 'other'. I'm sure that this awakening was the beginning of his awareness that some people were treated more equal than others."

Lillian and David Boyd Chase, parents of Jonathon "Skip" Chase, who loved to dress up and go out dining and dancing. Photo courtesy Linda Chase

Manhasset was a socially and economically variegated community. The "colored" lived in The Valley; blue-collar and well-to-do whites resided in Plandome; the well-off staked out Munsey Park, where the Chases lived. The only black people Skip knew were the maid Bessie, and her nephew, Reggie, who did occasional maintenance around the house. When he attended junior high in 1956, he became best friends with George, a black member of the wrestling team.

The parents were lively personalities who loved to dance and laugh and go to parties. This attitude of fun infused Skip and Linda with an outlook that marked their adult lives. Their father in particular gave them a love for seizing and controlling an audience with the force of personality. He could fine tune drama with masterful Shakespearean finesse, giving the play of life deep and colorful meaning.

Linda, who now lives in Manchester, England, has published four books of poetry, taught Tai Chi for twenty years, designed stage costumes and taught poetry. In her poem "Taffeta," she vividly captures her childhood home.

> *We heard her rustling down the stairs,*
> *drummer's brushes on a hi-hat cymbal*
> *and then on the lino the click and tap,*
> *of high heeled patent leather*
> *and the softer sound of dancing soles.*
> *She spun around like Cyd Charisse.*
> *Kids, how do I look?*
>
> *Her favorite dress, black and white taffeta*
> *with its New Look skirt needed crinolines*
> *to flounce the bottom out.*
> *Her charm bracelet jingled and Chanel No. 5*
> *Vied with our burgers and French fries.*
>
> *Then she did her 'I'm ravishing'* look,
> *pursed her lips, hand on her hip.*
> *Skip and I started to laugh, she laughed*
> *and Spotty yelped and wriggled.*

Then it was time for good night kisses,
    the I love you but I'm going out dancing *kisses*
    accounting for lipstick, hair, stocking seams.
We'd practiced other Saturday nights,
    Holding our arms out straight in the air—
    two little promises not to rumple or smudge.

We knew that children were not the only things
    on earth that counted.

The jitterbug did,
And the rumba.

The siblings relished a very close relationship from when Skip was given his one-day old sister to hold. "Skip was my protector, my hero, my mentor, my standard of excellence and the person I wanted to please most in the world," Linda said recalling her brother. "He walked me to school, got me up in the night to prevent me from wetting the bed, and rubbed my back in a darkened room when I had migraines. Surprisingly, he never made me feel as if I were a burden to him. That willingness to take responsibility was with him all his life, with me, with our pets and with family and career."

Skip and Linda attended a brother/sister camp near Albany for two months each summer for ten seasons, beginning at the ages six and four. Having a big brother look after her comforted Linda, who suffered from homesickness and spent many nights in the camp infirmary with physical ailments.

"Skip would come to visit me (in the infirmary) and talk through the rather crude mesh screens. He would bring me chewing gum from the trading post and slip sticks of it through holes in the

Linda and Skip at an early age (exact age unknown).
Photo courtesy Linda Chase

screen. I remember listening out for him before it got dark when he would come running along the path across the field."

A camp counselor, who later became Skip's colleague at the University of Colorado Law School, remembered Skip as "small, very active, a warm personable boy with a twinkle in his eye, always full of enthusiasm and with a full-speed ahead smile."

A lively, athletic boy, he attended public schools. In high school he became a talented and tenacious Greco-Roman wrestler. Not a big person, wiry and quick both on his feet and in his mind, Skip wrestled with a fierce sense of combative competition. In high school he also got into the ring of equal rights when he and fellow students went to the South and helped in voter registration during the Civil Rights movement.

The prestigious Williams College offered him a full wrestling scholarship, which he turned down although he did attend the school. He felt the scholarship should go to someone who really needed it, a reflection of his Robin Hood point of view, according to his son Adam.

Growing up in a wealthy environment might have fueled that Robin Hood sensibility. Not that Skip personally redistributed wealth, but he didn't take from those less fortunate. Because he had a maid didn't make him "better" nor did he feel a need to apologize for his circumstances: he came into that life because his father worked hard.

A second-generation Russian immigrant, Skip's father was a driven man toiling long hours building his New York City tax attorney service into a prosperous firm. (He changed the family name from Cohen to Chase in the late 1930s for the pragmatic reason he thought a more Anglicized name would serve him better in business.) Using his qualifications in accounting and law, David Chase became a specialist in designing tax-effective business mergers for clients.

"He was busy making the rich richer," Linda said. "He worked day and night, often arriving home late from the city only to retire into his study and work some more."

His personal sacrifice meant time away from the family and missing his son's wrestling matches. But Skip's mother attended every contest, her example giving him a strong family ethos.

Speaking of her mother, Linda said, "She crocheted, did pressed flowers, came to the football games to watch me and the other cheerleaders do our stuff. She made our house open to all, especially at Thanksgiving and Christmas and all summer long, since we had the only swimming pool among our group of friends. She was a committed member of the Congregational Church and became a major fundraiser for the church by organizing antique shows that become the biggest and best on all of Long Island. She raised funds for the Community Chest, ran flea markets for the American Cancer Society and set up a college scholarship fund for less well-off athletes. Plus, she was on the school board and a Girl Scout leader. Our mother had the biggest influence on Skip and me. She was completely committed to the well being of others. Later, Skip transformed that well being into legal rights."

Skip's son Adam credits his dad as a "great father who led by example. From him, I got the view of how I would be as a father. He and my mother instilled the value that if children are loved and made to feel they are the number one priority, not the only priority but the number one, that's all that matters."

Adam has three siblings: Tamara is an attorney; Rebecca works in New York in fashion and design; and Eli is a cyber-detective who helps police track down child pornographers. Rebecca, half-Korean, and Eli, half-black, were adopted. "My father would often bring home people he met on the streets, the way a child brings home a stray. Fortunately, we got to keep Rebecca and Eli," quipped Adam in typical Chase family humor.

"He'd take me to his rugby games and sit me by the keg while he played," Adam recalled. "When he was away at a game or skiing or on a bike trip, I didn't have the feeling, 'Oh, why isn't he with me.' I knew that as soon as he got back he would give the family his full attention, ask what we learned in school that day and what we did. When I was two or three years old, he'd take me to the gym's wrestling room and make me do bridges and exercises to give me a strong neck."

Lillian and David Boyd Chase in front of their home in Manhassat.
Photo courtesy Linda Chase

A strong neck is vital in wrestling; it's a wrestler's last great strength to prevent being pinned and losing the match. The resiliency of a strong neck, that bridge of determination and grit, keeps the shoulders lifted off the mat, a statement of, 'I'm not giving up. I'm not done yet.' A skilled wrestler can use a strong neck to orchestrate a reversal, snatching victory from an impending defeat.

"A strong neck is an important metaphor to understanding my father, as is wrestling." Adam looks very much like his father: dark hair, handsome, same body build and a quick warm smile. "Wrestling is an individual sport but it's also a team sport. An individual team member may win his match but if the team loses, the individual victory means nothing. Those lessons became a metaphor for me later in life, especially in law school."

Sitting in a conference room of the well-respected law firm where he works, Adam recalled, "There was lots of laughter in our home. Dad loved hearing any of us kids telling stories and jokes. My younger brother Eli has a photographic and phonographic memory, so he'd do great imitations. My father rejoiced in all that. We loved to tease him, although sometimes that wasn't the smartest thing to do." Adam, a runner who competes in international events, was wearing his normal office attire: t-shirt, shorts and running shoes.

Skip introduced Adam to a sense of social justice early in his childhood. "Many times I'd go with him to CRLS meetings and listen to the migrant worker issues. He and my mother raised us to know that our sense of family was not just the six of us, but extended into the community. As kids, we just assumed that everyone was part of our family."

This sense of family embraced Skip's law students, who treated the Chase home as their home away from home and as an informal classroom. "We had lots of students over," Adam said. "They just came in or stayed for dinner and there would be lively conversations. Dad liked to party with the students. In the classroom he maintained decorum but in our home it was more a family thing."

Skip also shared his sense of intellectual play with his family. "Dad would bounce things off me to get a lay person's point of view," Adam said. "When we were biking or running, he'd say, 'What do you think of this or that. Is it fair?' When I got older, he'd give me contract

The Private Man

Jonathon dressed for climbing, date unknown.
Photo courtesy Linda Chase

exam questions to see how I'd approach it. He wanted to know if the question was fair or not, and how I would answer it."

Skip met his future wife Nancy Markey while he was a student at Williams and she attended Bennington College. Seeing the dark-haired beauty from a distance, he was instantly smitten, although he didn't know her name or anything about her. In typical Skip fashion, he set about overcoming seemingly insurmountable obstacles—she had no idea who he was and was engaged to be married—by applying his considerable charm, a persuasive gift with words, glowing idealism that made his bright eyes even more vivid and total enthusiasm for life. He won her heart and they married directly after graduating from college.

The mate of a dynamic, high-energy person cannot be shy or a wallflower in order to hold his or her own in the relationship. Nancy matched Skip's energy and enthusiasm for life. She has a warm and generous heart equal, if not greater, to Skip's love of people. When he needed an intellectual foil, she parried and counterattacked to sharpen his argument. Friends and family admire Nancy for her honesty directly expressed and for defending her opinions with intellectual acumen.

"My mother gave as good as she got, with my dad or anyone else," Adam said.

She is credited, as a wife and mother, with being the glue that kept the family firmly bonded, especially as Skip's CRLS work often took him away for hearings and organizational meetings around the state. Her inherent Jewish motherness—fussing to make everyone comfortable, the love of family and children, good-natured cheer, insightful observations with an edge—made her, if not the den mother, then the cherished center of the tribe that gyrated around Skip.

"I give Nancy a lot of credit," said David Getches, a personal friend of the Chases and Dean of the University of Colorado Law School. "I'm reluctant to say this but Skip was not an easy guy to live with."

Magdaleno (Len) M. Rose-Avila, a close friend of Skip's and colleague at CRLS, honors Nancy. "I know how difficult it is on spouses when their mate is out trying to change the world." Rose-Avila has been a community activist, farm worker strike coordinator and worked with gangs in Los Angeles, El Salvador and Guatemala. "If you don't have a good partner in life, it's hard for you to do the creative things you need to do. A lot of us see the sacrifices Skip made but his family made a lot more sacrifices. They allowed him to do what he was doing. You look to the family and the sacrifices they make so the person can do their mission. That's the agreement for people like Skip doing outrageous things that put him in danger. The farmers, ranchers, didn't love legal services. They hated Skip. Hated everything he represented. He was putting his life on the line. But if he found that he would lose Nancy and the kids, he would have probably quit because he loved them so much. Nancy gave up a lot. She could have done more but because Skip was giving one hundred percent to his community, she concentrated on the kids and making sure they were sound."

Jean Dubofsky, a personal friend of the Chases, confirmed the high regard for Nancy. "Much of the cohesiveness of CRLS has to go to Nancy. She made all the people who came to Boulder to work for CRLS without family or friends feel that her home was their home, by inviting them in."

Dubofsky, who later became a Colorado State Supreme Court justice, was one of the first CRLS attorneys Skip hired. "I probably wouldn't be doing with my life what I'm doing now if it hadn't been for Skip," she said. "He gave me my first job in Colorado. I really didn't appreciate at the time what it meant to have an employer who wasn't threatened by a woman attorney, who hired her and treated her as an equal. Skip gave me and a lot of other young women attorneys a start on their professional careers. He affirmed, 'You are capable, you can do the job.'"

But Skip wouldn't have wanted to be deified. That glorification wasn't part of his ego package; he didn't think he'd look good in a halo. Demanding, impatient with those who couldn't keep up, he could be short, rudely so, even dismissive. "Brusque," is how fellow CRLS attorney Jon Asher described him.

University of Colorado rugby team, early 1970s. Skip is second from the left in front row.
Behind him, without a uniform, is Dan Israel, one of Skip's friends, if not his best.
Photo courtesy Maria Susan Aragon, Trudy Foreman and Jeff Aldred

"With Skip, you knew exactly what he was thinking and generally that was a positive. But there are times when diplomacy is the better tact. Let me put it this way; the really good golfers carry a big bag of clubs. Sometimes they need a driver, sometimes a wedge, sometimes a putter. I think it's fair to say that Skip went through life with one club. He had a driver. Sometimes, when you're on the green a little finesse and a little softer touch may get you farther than trying to put a forty-foot putt in with a driver. He wasn't just a hero. He was a pretty complicated guy in lot of ways."

He'd be so focused on his goals and interests, others—family and friends—felt they weren't getting the time and attention they needed. Driven like his father, Skip liked to laugh but he didn't find some things funny if it went against his grain. If you weren't with him, on his wavelength, friction could develop and he wouldn't necessarily think it was his fault. He tried people's patience, even that of his loved ones.

"Skip was always bewildered when opponents didn't like him," noted Jean Dubofsky. "Like all of us, he had periods when he thought he had no friends, that no one appreciated him. He always bounced back."

Sports—wrestling, rugby, lacrosse, skiing, biking, and running—were a life-long passion for Skip. The competitive and combative spirit of athleticism informed his nature. Even when sharing wrestling, running and biking with his son Adam, he didn't give away the game. "He'd complain if I couldn't keep up the pace on a bike ride," Adam remembered. "When we wrestled, it was more than a fun father-son roll on the floor. He wanted to teach me how to win, and that was by not losing himself. It was about doing your best effort, staying sharp, validating the self."

Combativeness and competitiveness share many traits—conflict, overcoming adversary, applying all your effort—but there are important distinctions. Being combative often has an extra edge that can become meanness, of having intent to physically and emotionally hurt; it doesn't carry a sense of play or an attitude of fairness. In combat, the goal is to conquer, perhaps humiliate, your opponent. Being competitive can imply play, even cooperation. Competing, top athletes force each other to up their game and perform beyond their personal best.

However, some CRLS attorneys resented Skip's competitiveness in "scooping up the good cases," according to Jon Asher. "There was a sense if you had a good case, don't let Skip know or he would take it and run with it. He was very aggressive. I frequently thought he didn't try to beat the other side, but to pin the other side as in wrestling. That was his style. Combative, very competitive, a little macho. While he was very bright, there were times when I thought he was impatient.

Rather than developing a case, he would file a case and hope he could develop it later. Sometimes he could and sometimes he couldn't."

Skip brought his spirit of competition into the courtroom. "He would not take on cases he thought he couldn't win," Adam said, "but winning was not always about what happened in the courtroom. Winning could be in raising an issue in the eyes of the public, bringing it forward for discussion or legislation or what might have a positive result in the community."

In her book *Deep Play,* Diane Ackerman wrote, "Most forms of play involve competition, against oneself or others, and test one's skills, cunning, or courage. One might even argue that all play is a contest of one sort of another.... To play is to risk; to risk is to play. The word *fight* derives from the word *play*. Medieval tournaments were ritualized battles that followed strict rules. So are wrestling, boxing and fencing matches."

This could well describe Skip's sense of play, including his approach to law.

Ackerman stated, "But when we peer even farther back into its origins, we discover that play's original meaning was quite different, something altogether more urgent and abstract. In Indo-European, *plagan* meant to risk, chance, expose oneself to hazard. A *pledge* was integral to the act of play, as was danger (cognate words are *peril* and *plight*.) Play's original purpose was to make a pledge to someone or something by risking one's life. Who or what might that someone or something be? Possibilities abound, including a relative, a tribal leader, a god, or a moral trait such as honor or courage. At its heart, *plegan* reverberated with ethical or religious values. It also contained the idea of being tightly fastened or engaged. Soon *plegan* became associated with performing a sacred act or administering justice, and it often appeared in ceremonies."

Skip Chase took risks as an activist lawyer with his career and his reputation in his play (plegan) with life.

"It (play) gives us the opportunity to perfect ourselves," Ackerman wrote. "It's organic to who and what we are; a process as instinctive as breathing. Much of human life unfolds as play."

Chapter 3

A Hoe, a File and a Clorox Bottle

Skip graduated from Williams College in 1961 with a Bachelor of Arts degree and received his law degree from Columbia Law School in 1964. After successfully passing bar exams in New York and Colorado (where his family often went on ski vacations), he took a job clerking for Federal District Judge William B. Herlands in New York.

But academics had always attracted him, and a year (1965-66) teaching at Boston University Law School confirmed his love for the classroom. "Our father was very disappointed in not having his son join him at J.K. Lasser in New York City," Linda said. "The story goes that he offered Skip twice the salary he would be getting in Boston. But Skip declined the offer."

In 1966, Skip accepted a teaching position at the University of Colorado Law School, where he taught until 1982, with one year (1977) as a visiting professor to University of Puget Sound Law School.

The move to the University of Colorado Boulder opened a new phase in Skip's professional life—he became a farm worker and an activist lawyer as well as a law professor.

In the 1960s, the University of Colorado's flagship campus, Boulder, was a hotbed of activism. Like many universities and colleges across the country, anti-Vietnam War, pro-feminists and civil rights movements inspired and enthused the student body to demonstrate against injustice, social wrongs and immoral profiteering. But the Boulder campus had an extra ingredient—an increasingly radicalized movement centered on the plight of migrant workers. The injustices they suffered symbolized the social and legal conditions of the general Hispanic, and the rural, poor community. The United Mexican-American Students (UMAS) and La Raza, a Chicano activist movement that evolved into a political organization, had a strong presence on the Boulder campus.

Members of the CU faculty were in the front ranks of the fight. Howard Higman, a young sociology professor, established the Colorado Migrant Council, with Bob Hunter, Tom Jones, et al, which first raised the battle flag over the potato and sugar beet fields. Son of a miner turned contractor, Higman was born in a hospital on the Boulder campus, where he spent his professorial life. As an undergraduate, he majored in art, switching to sociology in graduate school.

A brilliant man who considered his degree in everything-there-is-to-know and renowned for the breadth and depth of his knowledge, Higman loved to debate, provoke, challenge and jump into an intellectual fight with both feet. His most enduring legacy is the annual Conference on World Affairs at the University of Colorado, which continues to this day, attracting distinguished thinkers and doers from around the world for a week of public discussions.

The conference began in 1948 with a single-speaker tribute to the United Nations. The event proved so popular, Higman made it an annual gathering. In 1953, the conference drew national attention when Higman stacked the panels with speakers who attacked the tactics of Senator Joseph McCarthy at the height of his witch-hunting, anti-communist Congressional hearings.

In his distinguished career, Higman served on various government committees and four years as director of a VISTA (Volunteers in Service to America) training program.

"For all his quirkiness and his life style, Howard was a visionary of great import," confirmed Len Rose-Avila, who worked with Higman on the Colorado Migrant Council and with Skip at CRLS. "Howard determined there was a need for an agency to address farm worker issues. Because of Howard, Bob Hunter, Bill Prakken, and Skip Chase, CU had a lot to do with the movement in social justice in this part of the world."

Higman was already stirring the pot when Skip joined the university's faculty. Perhaps through Higman, he learned of the migrant farm workers conditions and found the cause to put his knowledge and sense of justice into action.

Skip believed that he needed to get his hands dirty, literally, before working for a people he knew little about, had no background affinity with and whose language he couldn't speak. In the summer of 1967, he worked in the sugar beet fields of northeastern Colorado and lived in the migrant labor camps in preparation for a fall semester seminar he planned to teach on law and poverty in rural areas.

Skip described his experience in the article, "The Migrant Farm Worker in Colorado—The Life and the Law", for the *Colorado Law Review* (1967, Vol. 40).

1. The Life
A. Delta, Colorado

Although it was still early in the morning, I could feel the sun burning a spot on my back through the hole in my tee-shirt. I straightened up, wiped my face with my already damp and dirty handkerchief and gazed down the long row of sugar beets—about a half a mile of them. Looking to either side, the beets on the eighty-acre field seemed to mock me, "You asked for it, baby, and here it is." The land beyond the field was treeless and flat, with only a farm house and an irrigation ditch making an occasional bump. Every once in a

A Mexican migrant farm worker weeding sugar beets near Brighton, Colorado. Photo taken in 1959. Denver Public Library Western History Collection, X-21639

while, a family on its way to church would make a trail of dust as it drove down the distant road. For some reason, that periodic passing of humanity only increased my feeling of desolation.

Hunched over, eyes down, looking for weeds (and they were everywhere), I made my way slowly, ever so slowly, down the row. There's one! Get it! I brought the hoe down again and again, harder and harder, against the tough root. My hands were already blistered from yesterday, and as the hoe came down short into the rocky soil it sent painful shivers through my body. Some weeds grew smugly right next to the beet; and, after having wiped out a small portion of the crop, I learned that it was almost hopeless to use the hoe in such a situation. I began reaching in to pull the weeds out with my hands. Some came out; others held as I pulled at them. New blisters were forming where the stalks had slipped through my grasp, and my hands had turned green. The sun continued to beat down on me.

After working for what seemed a long time, I looked up, expecting to be well down the row. I had made about twenty feet—twenty feet! The anger and frustration vented themselves as I came down harder and faster with the hoe.

At last the end of the row. "Don't walk back down the row for water," that lukewarm water sitting out in the sun in an old Clorox bottle. "Make yourself work back to it." "But I'm so thirsty." I started working back down the row. Towards the middle of the field, as I came down hard on a particularly tenacious weed, I heard and felt a familiar snap. It had happened yesterday, too; and I wasn't really sorry. The hoe had broken; I could leave the field! But what's the farmer going to say? Two hoes in two days? I began to realize that I must not be doing this exactly right. I had been working about six hours and had completed three and a half rows. At $8.50 per acre, sixteen rows to the acre, I had earned about $1.85, or $.30 an hour. I loaded my tools (broken hoe, rusty file, and Clorox jug) in the car, drove by George Hines' (my employer) house, and happily, finding no one there, left the broken hoe against a tree and headed back to my home—the Holly Sugar Labor Camp in Delta, Colorado.

A Hoe, a File and a Clorox Bottle

My hands were sore, I was hot, my house was filthy and I was in a strange town, doing strange work—badly—and living in a work camp where I was a curiosity. I was overpowered by a feeling of loneliness.

I had arrived at the Holly camp on Saturday afternoon, July 1, 1967. As I entered the camp office, George Hines, who grew sugar beets for Holly, was paying a family crew of Navajo workers. After tabulating their acreage, he made out a check, gave it to them, and they left the office. A few seconds after they had left, Mr. Hines turned to his son and asked him if that crew hadn't done a particular field, to which his son responded that they had. "We forgot to pay them for that," Hines said. "That's another hundred dollars we owe them." Whereupon he immediately left the office, brought back the crew leader, and made out a check for the right amount. My first preconception had been shattered within five minutes after arriving at the labor camp. I had expected to have things clearly and simply aligned the good guys against the bad guys, the worker against the farmer. Well, it wasn't that easy.

I very briefly explained my purpose to the manager and asked if I could stay at the camp. He explained that the camp was only open to people already contracted to work for Holly growers and that since I didn't have a job with a farmer growing sugar beets for Holly, I couldn't stay in the camp. I then turned to George Hines, who had overheard all of this, and asked him if I could work for him. I confessed I had had no experience weeding beets, that indeed, I didn't even know what a sugar beet looked like, but that I was sure I could learn to do it. He reckoned as how that was so and said he could use me. Now under contract to work for a Holly grower, I again asked the manager if I could stay. Not knowing quite what to do with me, he said that I could until he had an opportunity to check with his superiors on Monday. I was assigned a house and then drove out to the fields with Mr. Hines. Mr. Hines was extremely interested in my project and asked me several questions about it. Again Mr. Hines surprised me, because there was no suspicion or resentment whatever in his questions, only sincere interest plus tolerant amusement. In discussing the plight of the migrant worker I found Mr. Hines to have a real, although perhaps paternalistic, sympathy for his workers, referring to them over and over again as "poor things." His sympathy, however, had a fatalistic quality to it. It was a hard life, but that was the way it was—inevitably.

After a brief introduction to the beets, I was left alone in the field, working there for about three and a half hours until I broke my first hoe and returned to my new home.

The Holly Sugar Labor Camp is located in the northwest corner of Delta, just across the railroad tracks. Driving into the camp, one comes into a dirt lane lined on either side by large trees and five cinder-block houses, each containing two living units. About 150 feet to the south of the entrance road is another row of about five houses. At the east end of the entrance road is another row of about five houses. At the east end of this 150-foot clearing is a large aluminum washroom, and two hundred feet north of the central road stands another row of houses. This latter section was occupied by Spanish-American families and the remainder of the camp by Indians. With the exception of one family, all of the Indians were Navajo. I am sure the camp was rather attractive many years ago.

Even now, it is not too unpleasant, although the absence of grass anywhere gives it an overwhelmingly barren quality. (Why is it that migrants are denied the simple luxury of grass? In none of the labor camps that I visited this summer did I ever see a blade of grass—with the exception of a well-kept lawn surrounding the administration building of the Weld County Housing Authority in Ft. Lupton.)

My house was in the central part of the camp, in the Indian section. The inside had not been cleaned since last occupied (which had apparently been some time ago), and the former tenants had left a few open jars of pickles, chili, and other spicy foodstuffs, the rotting

Typical view of a migrant labor camp in Colorado. Photo taken in 1962.
Denver Public Library Western History Collection, z-777

smell of which permeated the place. The floor was thick with dust and particles of decaying food.

There were two rooms, each about twelve by eighteen feet. The front room contained a large wooden picnic table with benches, a double burner gas stove, some enamel cups and plates, a wash bowl, a frying pan and some eating utensils. (Only families were supplied with refrigerators.) In the rear room were about six army-type cots covered with stained, stinking mattresses.

I spent the first night in the camp sleeping in my car, ostensibly because the house was so stuffy, but really because I couldn't stand the filth and smell. Even after I cleaned the front room of my house and began to sleep there, I was sufficiently squeamish that I slept on an air mattress which I had brought rather than on one of the mattresses provided.

My source of water was a standpipe in front of the house which the children enjoyed playing with during the day, with the result that I usually had to vault a small moat when returning from work in the evening.

The central washroom contained his and her lavatory facilities. In the men's room there was a row of about twelve unenclosed toilets to the left and several basin-type urinals to the right. This room was filled with the stench more usually associated with outhouses.

There was another room containing sinks and laundry tubs, at the end of which was the entrance to the men's shower. The drain in the shower room was plugged and almost the entire floor was covered with water, thick with filth which one had to walk through to get to a shower. The stench from the lavatory found its way into the shower room and the combined smell of feces and putrid water rendered taking a shower almost intolerable. These, then, were the living quarters at the camp.

On Monday, during the noon break, I met Al Edwards, Holly's local field representative, whose role deserves explanation. Holly undertakes to supply the labor needed by its growers and does so by going through the Colorado Department of Employment, Farm Placement Service, which recruits for Holly in Texas and on the Navajo reservations. Once recruited, the labor either gets to Delta itself (with some financial help from Holly) or is transported in buses supplied by Holly (Indian labor is usually bused). The workers live in the Holly camp, Holly being paid a small amount for board by the farmers employing the labor. It is Al Edwards' job, among other things, to place the labor with particular growers and then to act as a go-between for the workers and the growers throughout the work period in beets—roughly from mid-May through late July or early August. The important factor is that once Holly has placed labor with a particular grower, Holly's direct responsibility ends. It is the farmer who arrives at the camp at 6 a.m. each morning to transport the workers without cars out to the fields, and who supplies them with hoe, file, and water. It is the farmer who drives the workers home every evening (perhaps stopping by a store on the way so that they may shop), learns his employees names, sees their children, sees where they live, and, when the section has been completed, pays them. The significance of this system will be appreciated when compared, below, to the contractor system utilized elsewhere in the state for furnishing labor not already placed and living with individual growers.

Al Edwards, aside from his role as farmer-worker intermediary, is also directly over the camp manager in responsibility for the operation of the camp. He came to see me on Monday to find out what I was doing at the camp, and then to determine whether or not I could stay. He was very personable and we talked easily, although he obviously had reservations about my presence. He explained that there was a policy against admitting single men (those traveling without families, either married or unmarried) because of a fear of drinking and the disquieting effect they might have upon the single maidens. I assured him that I was upright and that he had nothing to fear from me. When we parted, he was to check with his superior, Robert Ginn, the regional field representative, and let me know the verdict on Tuesday.

On Tuesday, Edwards told me that I would have to leave, reiterating the reasons given previously. (I had learned by this time, however, that other single men had lived and were presently living in camp.) I asked if I might speak to Mr. Ginn, myself, before having to leave, and this request was granted.

On Wednesday I went to the office of Robert Ginn in the Holly processing plant located near the camp. My demeanor in camp having been beyond reproach, I was sure that I would be permitted to remain. We discussed my being single and seemed to get over that hurdle. Ginn's next objection to my staying was that I was an Anglo. There were two races in the camp, he said, and that was already twice as much potential trouble as he wished. He specifically talked about the *possibility of someone picking a fight with me. This sounded absurd to me, although I am sure that to Ginn it was a very real fear. I had begun to make friends in the camp, and the last thing in the world that I felt was hostility.*

By this time, I began to realize that Edwards' and Ginn's misgivings about my presence were not really those which had been articulated, but rather concern about who I was and what I was really doing there. I had, of course, told both that I was an assistant professor of law at the University of Colorado School of Law, but had never thought to show any identification. Admittedly, I did not quite look the part of a professor. At my expense, we called the then Associate Dean of the Law School, James Buchanan, who verified my identity and purpose. After promising to stay out of the camp on Saturday night (that is when someone would be most likely to fight with me) and drafting and signing a waiver of liability in case someone should choose a night other than Saturday, I was permitted to remain.

Life in the camp soon became less lonely, thanks to a remarkable man named Frank Pebeahsy who befriended me early during my first week in Delta. I had found the Indians, in whose area of the camp I had been placed, to be rather wary of me. As mentioned earlier, there was no trace of hostility, but merely a bemused distance. I was indeed quite a curiosity. Children stared at me when I walked through the camp, and adults responded shyly to my greetings. Thus I was very happily surprised, when answering a knock at my door one evening, to find Frank had come over to say hello and talk with me.

Frank, as I said, is a remarkable man. He is Comanche, from Oklahoma, and married to a wonderful Navajo woman named Mary, who generously became my camp mother during my stay in Delta. He has completed high school, which is extremely unusual for a worker in the migrant stream, and both Frank and Mary speak perfect English, also unusual among the adult Indians. They have three sons living with them: Ronald, who is five; Frank, Jr., who is fifteen; and Adrian, who is seventeen.

Frank and Mary were regarded by most of the Indians in the camp, as well as by the camp manager, as the camp leaders. People went to them with their troubles, both domestic and those connected with work or the camp. I felt privileged and grateful to be their friend. During the two weeks I was in Delta, I spent many pleasant evenings either going in Frank's pick-up to the drive-in movies with him and his family, and usually a couple of other people as well, for some welcome entertainment, or just sitting around talking. My nickname was Custer, which I mention both because I am proud that they called me by a nickname and because it exemplifies their wonderful sense of humor that made being with them a lasting pleasure.

I must also mention the one incident involving the law. A girl of seventeen had been out with a couple who had been drinking heavily, although she had not. They asked her to drive their car home, and, although she had never before driven a car, she consented to do so. In the process, she wrecked the car, injuring the couple. She was arrested for careless driving and driving without a license, and faced a maximum of six months in jail and $10,000.00 in fines. We all expected the worst—or near to it.

The incident had occurred prior to my arrival in Delta, but I attended the trial. The court-appointed attorney asked the girl several questions, through a Navajo interpreter provided by the Colorado Migrant Council, in an effort to make sure she fully understood the charges against her and the nature of the proceedings. He asked here whether she wished to plead guilty or not guilty and she replied, "guilty." I was surprised since the attorney had done nothing in the way of a defense, did not appear to have advised her as to how to plead, and then did nothing, before sentencing, to bring out any extenuating circumstances. I was most amazed, however, when the district attorney recommended only a small fine and the judge sentenced her to pay twenty dollars, payable ten dollars a week out of her pay. This was as sensitive a handling of such a case by the court and the district attorney as anyone could have wished. The punishment was enough to teach her a lesson—for what she had done was serious—and yet was within her power to pay. Again, those from whom I had expected harshness had demonstrated mercy.

Migrant farm worker family harvesting sugar beets near Greeley Colorado. Denver Public Library Western History Collection, Llewellyn A. Moorhouse, Z-114

I worked the remainder of the first week for Mr. Hines. Having learned to keep my hoe sharpened by using the file regularly, I was able to move faster and to avoid breaking any more hoes. On Monday I had started getting company on my field. I was first joined by an Indian family working to my right. The mother, father and daughter worked, and a little boy about five or six stayed with them all day, entertaining himself as best he could by the side of the field. In an effort to give him an escape from the sun, the father assembled a rather ineffectual make-shift lean-to from a blanket and two short sticks. I always wondered why they didn't send the child to the school operated by the Colorado Migrant Council and finally, towards the end of the week, asked the father. Once he was able to understand my question, as he spoke very little English, he merely replied that they did not want to, that they wanted the boy with them. Perhaps this is another example of the Navajo suspicion of the white man.

Thursday afternoon we finished the first field and I was given a job on another small field belonging to Mr. Hines which was even weedier than the first. Working with me on this field were five men from Mexico who had only been in this country two years, and who spoke no English. They were traveling and working without their families and were living on the land of a farmer for whom they had been working.

On Thursday night it rained, and the ground was still wet when we came to work on Friday morning, soaking my boots and trousers as I worked down the rows, and causing the hoe to become heavily weighted with clinging mud. By 4:30 p.m., we had almost completed the field, only about six rows remaining to be done, when it began to rain again. That was it; we all started walking off the field. As we were leaving, Mr. Hines arrived to check our progress and was dismayed to see that we (actually they) were quitting. He had planned to irrigate the next morning and wanted the field finished that night, and implored us to stay. Since the men spoke no English and Mr. Hines spoke no Spanish, I used my meager Spanish and became the interpreter. It would have been all right had I only had to translate, but I found that I had to act as censor as well. The men wanted more money, Mr. Hines refused. The men said he was a cheap "son-of-a-bitch." Mr. Hines asked what they'd said, and I replied that they said he was careful about how he spent his money. Finally, all of us, including Mr. Hines, worked furiously together, finishing the field in about fifteen minutes.

Because the first field was unusually weedy and the second worse, Mr. Hines paid $10.00 per acre for the first and $1.40 per hour for the second. My wages for the first week, for about forty-two hours of work, came to $22.70.

On Monday of the second week, I began working with Frank Pebeahsy and his family and learned a few things about weeding beets. During the height of the afternoon heat, the beets wilt and all weeds rising above them must be cut down below that level. All others are ignored. My new savvy, plus the very important fact that that field was particularly free of weeds, enabled me to do two rows at a time, sixteen rows before lunch and another sixteen in the afternoon, two acres, $17.00 a day. Aside from the knowledge that I was making good money, I experienced a wonderful feeling of freedom and exhilaration in walking quickly and easily down the rows, flicking out now and then at occasional weeds. The anger, the frustration, the feeling of desolation was gone. Instead, I was out under the open sky, my own boss, making a good wage, working easily down a field abreast of my friend.

Our take for five days of work on that field was about $77.00 apiece. With three members of Frank's family working (Adrian was visiting his grandmother in Idaho), that is a living wage. If it were always like this, it would not be a bad life; but, as I had seen the week before, it was not—although conditions, generally, in Delta had been ideal. The weather had been almost perfect, with hardly any rain, there was plenty of work and not an oversupply of labor, and no contractor had taken anything in the middle.

Although now very much at home in Delta, I felt I ought to work in some other part of the state and, having learned from the farm bulletin in the Delta State Employment Office that ample work was available in Ft. Lupton, I decided that would be a good place to go. On Friday evening, I said goodbye to Frank, Mary and the children, each of us promising the other that we would meet again, and headed for Fort Lupton.

B. Fort Lupton

On Saturday, July 15, 1967, I arrived at the Fort Lupton Labor Camp, which is owned and operated by the Weld County Housing Authority and managed by a Mr. J. L. Rice. Until 1956, the camp was owned by the federal government, having been used during the 1930s as a CCC camp and during World War II as a concentration camp. In 1956 it was turned over to Weld County, under the United States Housing Act of 1937, to be used for low-income housing.

I first spoke to Mr. Rice about staying in the camp, merely saying that I planned to work in the fields and needed a place to live. He directed me to speak to a woman working in the camp office who, he said, would be able to tell me about the availability of housing. I was informed by this woman, whose name was Kathy, that the only housing open was for people who wanted to work pickles. I explained that I only planned to stay a week, to which she replied that in that case, there was nothing available, since I would have to be willing to stay for longer than that to get into the pickle housing.

I was aware that the Peace Corps had leased a large number of houses at the Fort Lupton Labor Camp in which to house and train over one hundred volunteers for service in Afghanistan. Hoping to somehow be squeezed into Peace Corps housing, I went to see Dr. William Griswold, the assistant director of the Peace Corps training program, and explained my objectives and my plight. He was extremely interested in my project and wished to help me if possible, and offered to speak to Mr. Rice to see if anything might be done. He was told by Mr. Rice that I ought to speak to Nato Martinez, a contractor in the camp, and ask him if I could work on his crew and live in one of the block of houses leased for him for his workers. I found Nato, and informed him that I was from the University of Colorado, wished to work with the migrants, and would like a job with his crew and a place to live. He asked me if I had ever worked sugar beets, to which

Ft. Lupton Labor Camp, where Jonathon lived and worked as a farm worker in the late 1960s. Photo taken in 1950. Denver Public Library Western History Collection, z-816

I, feeling rather pleased with myself, replied that I had, and was told that I had a job, beginning Monday morning at 6:30 a.m. He also told me that on Monday he would find me a place to stay, which he did.

The Fort Lupton Labor Camp contains about 210 living units, most of which are wooden frame structures, each containing one room about fourteen by sixteen feet in area in which up to six persons must eat and sleep. Army-type cots without mattresses, a small table about three feet square, one chair and a two-burner gas stove are furnished in each unit. Water is supplied by outside standpipes and there are central washrooms. On the whole, the camp was cleaner than the Holly camp in Delta, particularly the bathrooms. I was told, however, by several people who had been in the camp in prior years, that the buildings had been painted and repaired this year, with the arrival of the Peace Corps, whereas in the past years conditions were terrible. Even though cleaner, however, the facilities provided were far less adequate than those of the Holly camp.

A Hoe, a File and a Clorox Bottle

On Monday morning we drove to a farm north of Erie, about fifteen miles south of Fort Lupton, waited while Nato talked with the farmer and then drove out to the field of beets. Nato walked on the field, examined it, and came back and told us that the farmer was paying $.60 a row. The field was extremely weedy, but more than that, the ground was wet, the beets very small and chewed up by hail, and the rows appeared to have been planted by someone who'd had a bit too much to drink. They were crooked, with large gaps where there were no beets, and other sections where the beets became lost, running up into the center section between the rows. I am certainly no expert on agriculture, but the difference in appearance between the beet crop near Delta, where the fields are irrigated, and that near Ft. Lupton, where by and large the fields were not irrigated, was startling. Although we all grumbled about working on such a weedy field for $.60 a row, we began the task. At one point I asked Nato how many rows there were to the acre, to see if we were being paid the minimum set by the United States Department of Agriculture, and he said he did not know. We finished the field on Wednesday, working an average of about six hours a day. I completed twenty rows, earning $12; those working with me did not do much, if any, better.

The particular group that I worked with consisted of a grandfather, his son, his two grandsons, and a friend of the grandsons. They were, as were almost all of the people living in the Fort Lupton Camp, of Spanish-American descent and from southern Texas. The crews that I observed in the Fort Lupton area seemed to work shorter hours than those on the Western Slope, partially, I'm sure, because the crews in the East usually had their own transportation and were thus more mobile than those on the Western slope who were dependent on the farmer and his hours. I believe another reason for the shorter hours and, indeed, for a recognizably different attitude toward work, was the fact that the pay was so poor and the work so sporadic around Fort Lupton. There was little incentive to do anything more than earn

Migrant farm workers in a sugar beet field somewhere in Colorado. Photo taken October 9, 1960.
Denver Public Library Western History Collection, Z-771

enough for the next day or two, for it was hardly possible to save any substantial amount of money at $.60 or $.75 an hour, or even less.

When we finished the field on Wednesday, Nato informed us that he would have no more work until the cucumber harvest began, and that he did not know when that would be. Moreover, when I met Nato that evening to get paid he told me that Kathy had told him to inform me that I was to leave the camp. That day I had photographed a child of nine working in the field with us, an apparent violation of both state and federal labor laws, and Nato had mentioned this to Kathy. Since I'd planned to leave the following day I was not particularly concerned.

Wednesday evening I went with Jennifer Taylor and James Green, Head Start teachers in Fort Lupton working with the Colorado Migrant

Council, Roberto Valenzuela, a migrant worker and Marianno Ortiz, a former migrant and now a permanent resident of Fort Lupton, to a meeting of the Weld County Migrant Council in Greeley. Mr. Ortiz, who speaks very little English, had first mentioned the meeting, informing me that he was a member of the Weld County Migrant Council and that he would not attend any more of their meetings since no one cared whether he was there or not. He said he couldn't understand what was happening at them anyway. He did agree, however, that if the rest of us went he would go too.

In an interview with the Denver Post I was quoted as having said, as a result of this meeting in Greeley, that, "It (the Weld County Migrant Council) is composed of farmers and bureaucrats dedicated to maintaining the status quo." I went to the meeting at a time when people in the camp could not find work, and had not been able to for some time, and when food and money amongst the migrants had disappeared. The situation had become desperate, and I was anxious to know what steps would be taken by the Weld County Migrant Council to alleviate the terrible conditions.

Instead, the following transpired. The first topic of discussion was the relationship between the Weld County Migrant Council and the Colorado Migrant Council, the fear being expressed that the former might be subsumed within the latter. Next, representatives of the State Department of Education expressed concern over the fact that some children age five, who should have been attending the State operated schools, were attending the Head Start schools operated by the Colorado Migrant Council. The plain fact which emerged from this discussion was that these state educators were far less concerned over the welfare of the children than they were with seeing children, over whom they were supposed to have jurisdiction, go somewhere else. The last topic of discussion was the proposed stipend adult education program sponsored by the Colorado Migrant Council, whereby adult migrant workers, after the crops had been harvested, were to be paid to attend classes during the day in basic education, including reading, writing, and arithmetic. This program, although financed by the Colorado Migrant Council, could not be implemented in an area unless the local migrant council gave its blessing; and, in the case of the Weld County Migrant Council, where the farmers have a controlling voice, the program was rejected. One farmer at the meeting, with unabashed candor, remarked, "What are they (the Colorado Migrant Council) trying to do, educate these people so that they will be able to get better jobs and leave the fields?"

If this had been a meeting of the Farm Bureau or some school board, the display of insensitivity would have been disappointing; but that this is what happened at the meeting of a migrant council, a group supposedly established for the welfare of the migrant, was absolutely shocking.

I had made arrangements Wednesday evening to go out the next morning with Roberto Valenzuela to look for work. Roberto, 28, with a wife and three children, had not had any work for two weeks because of a hand injury, and by Thursday morning had absolutely no money and only a little flour left with which to feed his family. I went to his house in the labor camp at 6:30 a.m. Thursday morning to pick him up and was overcome, as I had never been before, by the terrible pathos of the way migrant families are forced to live. There, still sleeping curled around one another, were Roberto's three children, aged three, four and six, on a single army cot—with no mattress.

We drove over to the Brighton employment office, arriving a few minutes before it opened at 7:00 a.m. We told the man we would do any kind of work, and were directed to sit on chairs along the wall—and wait. During the next half-hour, four or five employees of the office and two other men looking for work arrived. After waiting for two hours with no work requests coming in, we headed back to the State Employment Office in Ft. Lupton.

A Hoe, a File and a Clorox Bottle

On the way to Fort Lupton, we stopped to talk to a crew topping onions, and they told us of a beet field west of Fort Lupton where workers were needed. Following their directions we got to an extremely weedy field with the longest rows I'd ever seen—about two-thirds of a mile—on which a family of four were working about two-thirds of the way down their first row. They told us that the farmer was paying $.50 a row and that it had taken them over an hour to get as far as they had. In other words, they were working for less than $.30 an hour. They planned to finish the row they were on, do one more back, and leave, earning just enough to get them by for another day or two.

Roberto and I left, went back to the Fort Lupton Employment Office, found out about another field, and went out and worked on it for about three and a half hours. Our combined take was $4.42. Roberto told me later that he and his wife went back to the same field on Friday and worked on a section containing shorter rows than on the section we had worked and made $1.83 between them for another three and half hours of work.

What had happened in Fort Lupton was that for several weeks workers had gradually been filling up the labor camp for the cucumber harvest which, however, was to be two to three weeks later than usual due to heavy rains, and had not yet begun. Beet work was almost finished, though a few fields remained to be done. The workers were hungry, they had no money, and the situation was ripe for exploitation.

Who was guilty of the exploitation? I cannot say for sure, but perhaps an explanation of the way contractors work will provide the basis for a calculated guess. Nato Martinez is typical of the labor contractor. He was himself, a migrant worker at one time and has now, in the best American tradition, turned entrepreneur. He contacts a crew of fifty or sixty workers in Texas and contracts with the Kuner-Empson Company to bring them up. Kuner-Empson, then, in addition to providing some financial aid in bringing the workers to Colorado, also leases a block of houses from the Weld County Housing Authority in which the workers live rent-free while working cucumbers. Prior to the cucumber harvest, when the people work beets, they still are allowed to live rent-free in housing leased by Kuner-Empson, the rent is paid either by the Great Western Sugar Company or by Kuner-Empson. Once the cucumber harvest begins, however, anyone living in Kuner-Empson housing must work cucumbers.

Prior to the cucumber harvest, during the periods when the migrants work beets—which is the period with which I have some familiarity—Nato finds work for his crew by being directed to growers through the Great Western field man, a counterpart of Holly's Al Edwards in Delta. That is the sole extent of Great Western's responsibility; all further arrangements, the most important being the rate of pay, are made strictly between the farmer and Nato. As mentioned earlier, when working for Nato he told us that the farmer was paying $.60 per row and that he didn't know how many rows there were to the acre. He also told me the farmer paid him $1.00 for each acre we did, which he indicated was the extent of his pay. Recently, however, I went back to see the farmer that I worked for on Nato's crew and learned some interesting facts, as did the farmer, whose name, I learned, is Carl Larson. First, Larson paid Nato $2.00 per acre, not $1.00 as Nato claimed. Second, Larson paid Nato $1.00 per row, not the $.60 which Nato paid us. Larson was unaware of the discrepancy, although he had made no effort to find out what we were actually paid. Third, on the particular field on which we worked, there were between nine and twelve rows to the acre, meaning that we got paid between $5.40 and $7.20 per acre, far below the minimum set by the Department of Agriculture of $8.50 per acre. That particular field contained thirty-six acres and approximately 400 rows, resulting in Nato's having received about $270.00 for our three days' work. Mr. Larson said this amount was more than the profit that he, the grower, would realize from the field.

In addition to the obvious economic disadvantage to the migrant farm worker incurred as a result of the exploitation by contractors, there is an economic disadvantage to the grower as well. I recall that Mr. Larson had been very dissatisfied with the job we had done on his field and it was not until I told him what we actually received that he understood why our work had been so sloppy.

Skip Chase speaking in Ft. Lupton during a ten-day fast. In the background are Tom Hewes, a VISTA volunteer; and Tep Falcon, an activist and wife of Ricardo Falcon, also a Chicano activist. Both Tom and Tep were part of a group of ten fasting to improve housing conditions in Ft. Lupton, Colorado. Photo taken in 1970. Denver Public Library Western History Collection, Z-826

Quite apart from tangible economic factors, the complete insulation of the farmer from his workers, as a result of the contractor, enables the farmer to treat labor as any other commodity, such as seed, which must be purchased at the lowest possible price. In Delta, on the other hand, the farmer was forced to respond to his workers as human beings, with the result that, in one area, the growers seemed to be genuinely concerned over the plight of the migrant and, in the other, conveniently blind and comfortably ignorant.

In an effort to alleviate, at least partially, the hunger in Fort Lupton, I called the Weld County Department of Welfare in Greeley to inquire into the availability of food stamps for these people. I was told that the head of each family should go to the Greeley welfare office to fill out the necessary forms, and that sometime during the following week a case worker would make an investigation. After another week or so, if the family qualified, the food stamps could be purchased. I suggested that I bring a busload of people over and was told that that would be quite impossible, that the forms were filled out in individual interviews, taking about an hour each, and that the size of the staff precluded accommodation of more than four families per day. Even should families qualify for the stamps, I was told, they would then have to pay an exorbitant amount to get them. For example, a family of six, earning $150.00 between them in the previous month, would have to pay $64.00 for food stamps entitling them to purchase $106.00 worth of food. The notion that members of a family being paid daily or bi-weekly should be able to save $64.00 out of $150.00 earned in a month is absurd. Fortunately, the Department of Agriculture also recognizes this, as I learned from a call to the Denver office, and instructs local welfare offices to certify that families be permitted to purchase stamps on less than a monthly basis, at intervals coincidental with when they are paid down to once a week.

After much prodding by migrants at a later meeting of the Weld County Migrant Council, the Weld county Welfare Department sent representatives to the labor camp in Fort Lupton where they spent almost two full days signing up families for food stamps. To my knowledge, however, no family was permitted to buy stamps more frequently than once every two weeks, which still rendered the program inaccessible to most inhabitants of the camp.

In late July, Vicente Ximenez, Chairman of the Inter-Agency committee on Mexican-American Affairs, conducted a hearing in Denver on the problems of migrant farm labor. Among those attending this hearing were several of the migrant farm workers from the Fort Lupton Labor Camp, myself, and representatives of relevant federal agencies in Denver, including the Wage and Hour Division of the United States Department of Labor. In 1966, the Fair Labor Standards Act was amended to cover agricultural employment for the first time, and, as of February 1, 1967, any employer of agricultural labor using more than 500 man-days of farm labor in any calendar quarter of the preceding calendar year was required to pay a minimum wage of $1.00 an hour. This is a protection in addition to the minimum piece-work rates set by the Department of Agriculture. Therefore, if the producer is covered by both Acts, the worker has his choice of the piece rate minimum under the Sugar Act, or the hourly minimum under the Fair Labor Standards Act, whichever is greater. Although most beet workers are aware of the minimum piece rates prescribed under the Sugar Act, none that I talked with had any knowledge of the hourly minimum prescribed under the Fair Labor Standards Act with the result that any compliance with the Fair Labor Standards Act by a grower paying at the piece rate was purely coincidental. When the piece rate yielded less than $1.00 per hour, compliance with the Fair Labor Standards Act was not demanded and it was certainly not offered.

We informed the representatives from Wage and Hour that everyone working out of the Fort Lupton camp had received less than the hourly minimum wage and they asked that complaints be filed by those then present for back wages. I left at that time, assuming that action was to be taken. About two weeks later I called Wage and Hour and learned that no complaints had been filed and that nothing was being done. I suggested that they had received enough information to warrant their undertaking their own investigation and was told that that would be impossible without complaints. I explained that since the workers did not know the names of the farmers for whom they worked, any complaints would have to be made against the contractor, and it was unlikely that anyone would file against a contractor since the workers were dependent on him for work and housing. I was told that names of complainants would be kept confidential, but it is unlikely that workers would believe that. Furthermore, the people in the camp had very little faith in filing complaints and thought it foolish to take risks when the likelihood of any satisfaction was extremely remote.

One apparently simple solution to the problem of the migrant farm worker is for him to stay in one place and get a non-farm job. Let me describe, however, the difficulties encountered by Roberto Valenzuela when he tried to do just that. Roberto's education ended with the second grade, which immediately excludes him from most of the better jobs. He had had experience, however, as a truck driver in Texas, and when interviewed in a state employment Office in Denver, where he went to look for a permanent job, he informed them of this experience. He was told that unless he could produce references from Colorado employers for whom he had driven, he could not be referred to anyone for a position as a truck driver. Since this was obviously impossible, he was told that he would hear, within a few days, about opportunities for factory work in Denver. After almost two weeks had gone by with no word from the employment office, I offered to call to see what had happened. I was informed that factory jobs were very scarce and that there was little possibility in getting one unless Roberto was to come to the office each morning. Because it was necessary for Roberto to get whatever work in the fields he could, and because of the time and cost of driving to Denver, this could not be done.

Next, Roberto tried to get a house in the permanent housing section of the Fort Lupton Labor Camp. He was first told that such housing was only open to persons who had lived in the area for six *months or more, a policy which effectively excludes all migrants wishing to remain. He was later told, however, after obtaining a job with the Colorado Migrant Council, that when the Peace Corps vacated the permanent housing it was occupying, he could have a place. In the meantime, however, he had found another place to live. A Mr. Hernandez, however, was not so fortunate. He also wished to stay in Fort Lupton, had a job through February, but was not permitted to stay in the permanent section of the labor camp; no reason was given for his rejection.*

During the period before Roberto located a residence, he attempted to enroll his oldest boy in the Fort Lupton public schools, but was told that as long as he continued to live in the migrant section of the labor camp, his son would have to attend the special migrant school between Brighton and Fort Lupton, where Spanish is used extensively in teaching. Roberto, however, was very anxious that his boy learn to speak English and, for that reason, that he attend the regular public schools. But he couldn't.

When Skip left the Ft. Lupton labor camp, he stopped by the office to inquire about the reason for his eviction. He asked why families living in the camp could not be furnished with mattresses and decent-sized tables. "They (the workers) would slash the mattresses and break the tables," he was told. "Yet I had just come from Delta where these were supplied and were not destroyed. Furthermore, a new camp built last year in Manzanola has met with such great success that a group of farmers in nearby Granada have constructed another new camp this year, consisting of seventy-two units. The truth is that when good housing is provided, it is cared for; unfortunately, the attitude expressed by Kathy in Fort Lupton reflects the attitude of all too many people in this state, which attitude becomes the excuse for providing wretched housing. And, when wretched housing is provided, it is cared for accordingly, thus further entrenching erroneous preconceptions."

Chapter 4

Bringing Law to the Fields

After his summer in the fields working along side migrant workers, Skip returned to CU determined to do more than just teach a class on the legal and social injustices suffered by migrant workers and the rural poor. But it wasn't until he met Bill Prakken that the Colorado Rural Legal Service became a reality.

Prakken graduated from the University of Michigan Law School in 1967. Social justice was an abiding interest—he considered joining VISTA—so rather than climb the corporation legal ladder, he won a Reginald Heber Smith Community Lawyer Fellowship, awarded by the War on Poverty Legal Service as a way to compete with large law firms for talented young lawyers.

"I was in the first class, only fifty of us," Prakken explained at the law firm in Grand Junction, Colorado, where he worked for years before going into semi-retirement. A soft-spoken man, his laid-back persona hides a sharp legal mind and a spine of steel when it comes to negotiations: he was the man other CRLS attorneys called in to handle difficult situations. "We were given a month's training in poverty law at the University of Pennsylvania and then assigned to different projects around the country. I was sent to Pueblo, Colorado. While in Pueblo, it struck me that Colorado, with its rural communities and migrant workers, could use a program similar to the California Rural

Legal Assistance (CRLA), which was doing great things in the rural areas of California with migrant workers."

Through the lawyer network, he learned of Skip at the University of Colorado in Boulder. "I had gone to Williams College for my freshman year and knew Skip's name, although he was a couple years ahead of me." By then, Prakken had left Pueblo after a year and was working for the highly regarded Denver law firm Holland and Hart. After several visits and discussions with Skip, Prakken decided to leave his law firm, "which was useless as far as poverty law was concerned," including the comfortable income it provided, and join Skip in Boulder. "We were hoping to use Skip's affiliation with CU as a part of CRLS."

The two young idealistic attorneys became best of friends. They shared a strong motivation to make things better for folks, liked to party and ride motorcycles to Denver for meetings. "I have a very vivid picture of him," Prakken remembered, "from the time we were putting the CRLS proposal together. We were over at the CU Law School. I was at the far end of a corridor and he spotted me and came running as fast as he could to me. He was very charming, very smart, anything but a saint. I considered him one of my best friends."

Prakken filled out the application for an Office of Economic Opportunity (OEO) grant for federal funds to the Colorado Legal Rural Services as a charitable and educational organization whose purpose is "…specifically to organize, establish, and carry out a program providing full legal services to indigent persons in various regions of the State of Colorado and to otherwise promote the general welfare of poor persons in the State of Colorado."

"We sent in the application and did some lobbying. One of my Michigan classmates, Mike Davis, a fellow Reggie, as the recipients of the Reginald fellowship were called, was working in the national

Bill Prakken, co-founder with Skip Chase of Colorado Rural Legal Services. Year of photo unknown. Photo courtesy the Prakken family, Grand Junction, Colorado

office of legal services at the time. In those days there was a fair amount of money out there for the War on Poverty and legal services and other federal programs."

Skip, showing political savvy, added a sweetener to the grant application—he included Len Rose-Avila, then working with the Colorado Migrant Council.

"When we received the grant, I became involved full time as the acting Deputy Director," Prakken said. "There was just the two of us. We hired Linda Head as the office manager and Len Avila as a community organizer."

Rose-Avila, who became Skip's personal friend, said, "Once, he co-signed a note for me to buy a GTO. Occasionally he'd call and say, 'Len, the bank called me about the missing payment. Is it coming in?' I'd reply, 'You've got to have faith, Skip.' And he'd answer, 'We're thirty days beyond faith.' With CRLS, he wanted to show that he had a Latino who would work with the program, so asked if he could put my name and resume in the proposal."

Like many of Skip's hires, Rose-Avila was a quality activist. Son of Mexican immigrant parents and one of 12 children, he knew first-hand the migrant worker experience. At the age of 11 he was thinning onions in the fields and two years later worked as a full-time migrant field hand following the vegetable and fruit crops around the western United States.

"I was supposed to enroll into San Diego State, but my 14-year-old sister was put into the Good Shepherd Home for Girls, a Denver correctional school, by the welfare department for 'acting out.' " (She was later diagnosed as manic-depressive.) I came to Colorado to help her and applied to the University of Colorado, 30 miles from Denver, so I'd be close to her. I had no money for tuition or housing. After I was accepted, I spent two weeks before classes sleeping in my car in a school parking lot before some Anglos invited me to stay in their dorm room."

He co-mingled his studies with activist work: served as the Colorado Migrant Council regional office director in Greeley, Colorado; taught for Head Start in Granada, Colorado; organized workers in the field camps in Ft. Lupton, Colorado; was a leading figure in the Chicano movement and ran for public office as the La Raza Unida Party's candidate for Colorado's Secretary of State.

In his later career, Rose-Avila ran congressional campaigns and worked for the Democratic National Committee, taught theater and sociology at CU, and sociology at Colorado College. He's held various administrative and leadership positions in Amnesty International USA and was the inaugural Executive Director of the Cesar E. Chavez Foundation. He also served as the United States Peace Corps Country Director in Nicaragua, Guatemala, Paraguay and the Federated States of Micronesia and Palau. Currently, he is the Executive Director of the Northwest Immigrant Rights Project in Seattle, Washington, until his retirement.

The Colorado Migrant Council advocated in the fields for better working conditions, fair wages, education and housing for migrant workers. "We'd go out and find discrimination in pay, housing, employment, pesticide use and were doing social justice work around those issues," Rose-Avila said.

Lobbying state agencies and the state legislature to correct the unjust, and often illegal, practices brought no results. "One of our frustrations was the lack of a legal service program," Rose-Avila said of those times. "When I grew up as a farm worker, there were two things we prayed for: one was to have medical clinics and the other to have attorneys to sue people with. So when Skip, working on his own, recognized the need for CRLS we were all excited. He was the mother, father and mid-wife to CRLS. Skip and CRLS was the reason for the later successful farm workers strike in Center, Colorado, I organized. His support made it possible."

After hiring Rose-Avila as CRLS's first Latino employee, Skip wasn't bashful about parading him out whenever it proved useful. When OEO officials visited the Boulder CRLS office to evaluate the program for future funding, Skip told Rose-Avila, "I want to show you off to the Washington people."

"So when the day came, Skip called me into his office. I took off my white shirt and, wearing a t-shirt, grabbed a waste bin on wheels and stuck a feather duster in my back pocket. I opened his office door and began dusting. 'Oh, Senior Skip, did I come in at the wrong time?' I said in a humble Mexican accent. 'You want me to come later and clean, patrón?' He told me to get out, 'Out of here now!' He was so mad he called me every name but Mexican and didn't speak to me for several days."

Remembering his friend, Rose-Avila said, "Skip never understood his place ethnically or racially. He was a Jewish Chicano who knew the difference between right and wrong. He went to radical demonstrations lifting his fist and shouting, 'Viva La Raza!' He willingly took his hits right along with the rest of us, quite often as a sacrifice to himself and his family. He was a human rights activist and a good attorney who believed that justice delayed is justice denied. We'll never forget the obstacles that were removed, the paths cleared, the doors opened by Skip. He built a foundation that changed our lives and the lives of many others.

"Skip was very much a humanist. He really cared about me and the other people he worked with and their wellbeing. A couple of times I jumped off more than I should have jumped off. He basically told me, 'Don't jump unless you really need to because you'll get yourself in trouble.' I was doing some things and saying some things that could have hurt me in the long term and hurt the people I was working with. He was very conscious of that. I thought, 'Who's this white guy to lecture me?' But it was very good that he told me that. It made me think. I admired his counsel. If he hadn't cared about me, he wouldn't have told me. But he cared enough. Not many people would have taken a chance with a crazy person like me."

Rose-Avila wasn't Skip's only politically smart choice in launching CRLS. For the first board members, he chose a broad spectrum including Latinos and ranchers. "I told him that by choosing some of those people, particularly the conservative ones, he was selling out," Rose-Avila said. "He explained that he needed them for cover to go argue for the middle of the road so CRLS could do the radical stuff."

Board members came from the Legal Aid Society in Denver, non-lawyers, attorneys from different parts of the state, such as John Roach in Grand Junction, and Bill Cohen.

A former Washington D.C. federal prosecutor, Cohen was on the CU Law School faculty with Skip. They became fast friends and their families often celebrated the Jewish holidays together. Cohen first brought Jean and Frank Dubofsky to Boulder, which impacted CRLS in ways neither man anticipated at the time. Jean became a lead attorney at CRLS and filed important cases with Skip. Cohen knew her husband, Frank, who also worked for CRLS, from Georgetown Law School. He invited Frank to join the Legal Aid and Defender program Cohen started to provide legal services for indigent people, an urban version of the rural CRLS.

"Skip saw that I had knowledge and expertise that could be useful to CRLS," Cohen said recalling those days when he and Skip were 29-year-old law professors not satisfied being confined to the classroom. "He was very astute in choosing members of the CRLS board," a harbinger of Skip's political adroitness in finding board members who broadened the CRLS support base.

However, the choice for the first Chairman of the Board, Dave Miller from Greeley, Colorado, wasn't a sure step. "He was an older guy who had a hard time with some of the CRLS goals," Prakken said. "Some philosophical questions, but more how the program was to be administered and run. What we were doing. It was awkward for a while. In dealing with Miller's personality, both Skip and I felt like ducking for cover. Just because we were the co-founding members didn't give us any special treatment with him. But, he resigned after a short time."

Skip was the public face of CRLS, the fire'em up guy. Prakken, who had more practical law experience—by a year—stayed in the background doing the nitty-gritty work. "Skip was a lot of things but he was not a particularly good trial lawyer or even an appellate lawyer for that matter," Prakken said in all honesty of his friend. "There was a time when Skip got worked up about an injustice and exclaimed, 'We've to get a restraining order.' He sat at a table with a group of CRLS attorneys around him and wrote a few words, then stopped to think and wrote a few more words, then stopped again. Finally, he looked up and asked, 'What's a restraining order? How do you write a complaint?' The other lawyers didn't know either. Many were too inexperienced or that was not the type of law they practiced. They called me in and I wrote the complaint."

CRLS cabbage-green attorneys made "countless mistakes" in the beginning, according to Prakken. "But, by and large, the judges recognized we were not trouble makers necessarily and they dwelt with us pretty well. I remember a mistake by one of our attorneys, Jerry Reese. He showed up in court not wearing any socks. The judge, Jim Kerr, an old guy, blew up at Jerry. But I think the quality of the people we had working was pretty high and we did fairly well overall."

Skip and Prakken started hiring staff after setting up the CRLS office in the abandoned St. Gertrude Academy, formerly a Catholic elementary school, courtesy of CU. "We painted the walls ourselves," Prakken remembered with a smile. Part of his job was also to travel around the state establishing other CRLS offices.

Bringing Law to the Fields

St. Gertrude's Academy in Boulder, Colorado where the first Colorado Rural Legal Services office was housed in 1969. Photo by George Ron Waldie

"We were hippy lawyers," Prakken said. "We all had suits and ties when needed but wore our hair long and drawn back. Jean and Frank Dubofsky's place up in the mountains on Wild Tiger Road could be described as a hippie pad. My wife, Judy, and I lived a couple mountains over from them. Periodically, CRLS would bring all the lawyers into Boulder for educational sessions. Afterwards, we'd have a big party, often at our house. I remember getting up in mornings and there'd be bodies sleeping all over the place. I'd be stepping around them wondering who most of them were.

"The first CRLS attorneys were young and mostly inexperienced. Often times one of the lawyers would be doing their first case. Some of them, like John Kuenhold, were in the VISTA program and assigned to us. We all came to CRLS with a lot of ambition to do great things, to change the landscape, change how low-income people were treated in jail. Everyone was looking for impact cases, cases that would have an effect beyond the controversy our individual client was involved in. What we brought to the communities was the fact there would be a voice for someone and that in itself brings benefits. The law allowed you to get a fair hearing to determine whether or not one was guilty or innocent."

Could the CRLS program be founded in present-day context? Cynics give a big raspberry at the very suggestion. In this climate of "me-ism" when law students are chiefly concerned with landing a corporate job with a career path leading to big bucks? Forget about idealism, the fledgling lawyers have big student loans to pay back.

The social and political activism of the 1960s did lend impetus to the establishment of socially conscious organizations such as CRLS. The 1960s "hippies" pushed back against the values of the 1950s, a decade when the nation wanted comfort and security after fighting World War II and the Korean War. The Eisenhower era was a time for returning veterans to establish themselves, get an education, land a solid job or start a business. They had had enough of turbulent seas and wanted a stable boat for their life's journey.

But their children—the troops of the anti-Vietnam War and the Civil Rights movements, the "flower-children" who led a sexual revolution, those spawns who became defying musicians and artists, those idealists who gave themselves of anti-poverty programs and Head Start, a pre-school program serving primarily the disadvantaged, and VISTA and legal aid services—they were determined to upset the apple cart of staid acceptance.

On the national scene, Martin Luther King led marches demanding racial equality; President Lyndon Johnson declared a War on Poverty and pushed the Civil Rights Act through Congress; Congress established the Peace Corps and Office of Equal Opportunity, which funded programs such as Head Start and CRLS and VISTA. It was a time of national optimism when the young people took to heart President John Kennedy's ringing declaration, "Ask not what your country can do for you, but what you can do for your country."

The 1960s generation of longhaired "freaks" no longer accepted the corporate dictum of profit above all else. The organization man with his button-down collar and neatly trimmed hair became their straw man. Jimi Hendrix, Janis Joplin, The Beatles and The Rolling Stones replaced Frank Sinatra and The Andrews Sisters.

Activist lawyers took the Chicago 7 case when seven anti-Vietnam War activists were arrested and charged with conspiracy and intent to incite a riot during the 1968 Chicago Democratic National Convention. Their lawyers argued that the anti-riot section of the Civil Rights Act of 1968, under which the defendants were indicted, violated their clients' First Amendment rights. After an infamous trial, the defendants were found guilty (later reversed) and sentenced to five years in prison and fined $5,000 each.

Philip Gourevitch, in a *New Yorker* article, made the point "... humanitarian that emerged from Biafra—and its lawyerly twin, the human-rights lobby—is probably the most enduring legacy of the ferment of 1968 in global politics. Here was a non-ideological ideology of engagement that allowed one not to be identified with power; to stand always with the victim, in solidarity, with clean hands...."

(In 1968, the oil-rich province of Biafra seceded from Nigeria. The national government laid siege on the renegade province. In the ensuing civil war, the state government used starvation as a legitimate tool of war, the result being the death of thousands of children. Photos of the cadaverous, swollen-bellied, stick limbed children aroused world sympathy and an outpouring of humanitarian aid.)

"...a non-ideological ideology of engagement that allowed one not to be identified with power; to stand always with the victim, in solidarity, with clean hands...."

Skip Chase could have been a poster child of his times.

"My father was a Kennedy liberal," Adam said. "I don't think there were any Republicans in our family, except for my grandparents and they didn't stand on a political soapbox. The political discussions around our family dinner table were preaching to the choir. My dad was too young to be a beatnik and too old to be a hippie, even though he went through a phase of wearing beads and turquoise jewelry—even in the classroom. He also played the bongos."

Optimists point out that idealism is alive and well and always will be. Legal services around the country thrive. The Colorado Legal Service (which absorbed CRLS in 1999) is active throughout the state.

David Getches, former Dean of CU Law School, reflected on Skip's influence on the school's tradition of activism. "He was a vibrant part of a tradition that preceded and followed him, and he ignited the goals that we are proud of having all along. During that period, if you didn't chip in, if you didn't help solve the problem, you were part of the problem. It was really critical to have Skip give meaning to our program and to lead the students—to give them a good loft to their inclination to try and make things better.

"A continuing cultural definition that impresses me is the ideal of public service, of having to do something for society. That we as lawyers are servants, we are here to try and make things better and to solve problems. There are students here who think they can make a lot of money as a lawyer. But, over the years I've been here, a long time, I see a predominance of students who want to do public service. Two years ago our students championed a pro-bono pledge program. If they do fifty hours of public service, they get a notation on their

David Getches, former Dean of the University of Colorado Law School. David was close friends of the Chase family, and consulted with Skip when founding the Native American Rights Fund (NARF) in the 1970s.
Photo courtesy the University of Colorado Law School

transcript. They cannot get money for it or credit. We, as a law school, could not do such programs if it wasn't in the hearts of our students."

The CU Law School instigated one of the first legal clinic programs in the country, starting in the 1950s. "A legal clinic is an expensive form of education, to have only a handful of students in the program," said Getches in his office. A tall lanky Westerner, his legal specialties were water law, public land use, environmental law and Indian law. Originally form California, he and his wife arrived in Boulder in 1971 to establish the Native American Rights Fund, which is how he met Skip—seeking legal advice to set up a non-profit legal service in Colorado.

"The head of our legal clinic program, Norm Aaronson, limits his clinics to ten students to one professor per semester. In a regular class there are eighty or so students, so our dedication to resources is much greater for clinics. We started making legal education more practical through the clinics, but that needs to expand because law firms and public agencies no longer commit the investment of training young lawyers how to do it. They expect more preparation coming out of the law schools. Skip was doing that early and he was doing it between the clinical program and the academic program. He'd use his Constitutional Law class like a clinic. He got students involved."

Chapter 5
San Luis Valley

Google Earth's view of the San Luis Valley with the Sangre de Cristo Mountains and Great Sand Dunes on the right (east) and the San Juan Mountains on the left (west). The small farming towns affected by CRLS—Alamosa, Monte Vista, Del Norte, Center and Sagauche—all rest in this expansive valley

Skip took a leave of absence from his teaching duties at the University of Colorado Law School to establish CRLS. Within two years, CRLS offices were functioning in Greeley (sugar beets) in northeast Colorado; Grand Junction (fruit) in the western part of the state; La Junta and Trinidad (farming and ranching) in southeast Colorado; and Alamosa (potatoes and lettuce) in the San Luis Valley.

The San Luis Valley became, along with sugar beet farms around Greeley, the most contentious of CRLS's programs.

The San Luis Valley, an extensive alpine valley (average elevation 7,500 feet) sitting atop the Rio Grande Rift, is a true desert, receiving about eight inches of rain annually. Yet, it supports an extensive agricultural industry of potatoes, head lettuce and barley.

In the 1960s, approximately 40,000 migrant workers, primarily Mexicans, Mexican-Americans and Navajos, worked in the valley during harvest season. The people needed work and the farmers depended on them to bring in the labor-intensive potato and lettuce crops. But an undercurrent of economic competition made the symbiotic relationship an uneasy alliance: the workers needed fair wages and decent housing and the farmers needed to keep their expenses down, which often meant cutting labor costs.

The situation encouraged exploitation and unfair practices, exactly what Skip Chase dedicated his legal career to fight.

The San Luis Valley (SLV in local shorthand) was part of Mexico until ceded in 1848 to the United States after the Mexican-American war. Spanish influences—food, language, and culture celebrations—are a strong presence in the valley today. In 1849, the Kapota band of Ute Indians, who used the valley as a summer hunting ground, made a peace treaty with the United States government but was forced to relocate in 1868 to a reservation in western Colorado. However, the Native Americans hung on to land in the northwestern corner of the valley until the Meeker Massacre in 1879 wiped out their presence.

Today about fifty percent of the valley is privately owned; much of the extensive ranches were part of Spanish and Mexican land grants dating back hundreds of years.

San Luis Valley

There are two main accesses to the San Luis Valley: straight south from Salida on state highway 285; or south on I-25 from Pueblo to Walsenberg, then west on U.S. Highway 160 over La Veta Pass. Either way, the valley is a stunning experience.

Bordered by the San Juan Mountains on the west and the Sangre de Cristo (Blood of Christ) range on the east, the flat expanse of the 112-mile long and 74-mile wide wishbone-shaped valley is the epitome of the wide-open West. "Chico brush"—rabbit brush, greasewood and other low brush—spreads across the valley floor. Meandering lines of cottonwoods mark the occasional watercourse. Bosky canopies shelter widely spaced farmhouses and ranches from the summer's scorching heat and the winter's bone-chilling winds. The small towns linked by two-lane asphalt roads are delineated by clumps of greenery.

But, it's a mistake to take the valley's Western scene as bucolic. New York passions charge the small towns; Washington D.C. distrust and back stabbings rankle; jealousies and revenge and disloyalty blue the air; and racial dislikes rooted in centuries of prejudice flit like mirages.

The most notable feature of the San Luis Valley is the immense, even intimidating, space. The mountain ranges, often no more than a jagged low line on the horizon, give a sense of containment, but nothing contains the other dimension of the valley—the space above. That tetragrammatonic sky, infinite in depth and breath, invokes inspirational joy, ethereal rapture, fearful wrath, the overwhelming sensation of humility and is the source of myths and legends.

Several southwestern Native American tribes regard the San Luis Valley as a sacred location, specifically the San Luis Lakes area known to the tribes as Sipapu, the place of emergence. In their belief system, just before a catastrophic "cleansing" of the earth heralded by natural upheavals and changes, the tribes are to be led to safety underground at Sipapu. The Navajo (the Navajo Nation lies south of San Luis in New Mexico) hold that our current time is the period of the Fifth World, with only two worlds remaining above this realm: World of the Spirits of Living Things and Place of Melting into One. The end of the Fifth World will be announced by sky katchinas—perhaps in the form of fireballs—that signal the time to travel to Sipapu, in order to survive the coming cataclysms, is at hand. Once underground, the tribes will be cared for by ant people for several generations until it's safe to re-emerge and re-populate the new world.

Blanca Peak, in the Sangre de Cristo range, is the "sacred mountain of the east" (Sisnaajini) where, according to Navajo legend, star people entered our reality aboard flying seed-pods. The Navajos aren't the only ones who associate flying "seed-pods" with the region. UFO sightings have been reported in the San Luis Valley since the 1930s. (The area lies on the western edge of a scientifically proven maximum-intensity aeromagnetic zone.)

In the 1950s green fireballs streaking across the sky were reported by thousands of people across southern Colorado and northern New Mexico. Robert Whitting, a local Episcopal minister, publicly insisted he had been in telepathic contact with beings operating a craft that flew next to his car. The friendlies warned him of a large animal on the road and he was able to swerve around a large black dog lying dead on the highway.

The valley has also been the site of mysterious animal mutilations associated with aliens probing our world, the most famous being Snippy the Horse. Dead Snippy was found with all the tissue from the tip of her nose to her shoulders missing, and minus her heart and brain. A strange medicinal ordour hung about the corpse for days, according to reports, and eighteen-inch "giant, horse-like tracks" ended about 100 feet from where Snippy lay.

"Flying saucers killed my horse," declared Snippy's owner, Nellie Lewis. "They'll come out in force one day."

For several years in the 1970s dozens of valley ranchers reported mutilated livestock, the circumstance suggesting some kind of experimentation. This was during a time when hundreds of cases of mutilated animals and strange aircraft hovering over the sites were reported in the United States and Canada.

Another anomaly of the San Luis Valley is the sand dunes at the base of the Sangre de Cristo Mountains. Covering 40 square miles, some dunes rise to 750 feet above the valley floor, the tallest dunes in North America. They were formed in the mid-Holocene era 8,000 to 5,000 years ago, according to geologists, and were again active in the late Holocene 3,500 to 1,500 years past. Much of the sand was derived from volcanic rocks of the San Juan Mountains and deposited by the Rio Grande River in the river's huge alluvial fan on the western side of the valley. Prevailing southwesterly winds blew the sand sediment across the valley, piling it against Sangre de Cristo's flank.

When John Kuenhold, accompanied by Skip, first entered the San Luis Valley, he drove past the Great Sand Dunes National Monument. On that summer day, Kuenhold didn't realize he was stepping into a future that would keep him in the Valley more than forty years. (Presently, he serves as a Chief Judge of the 12th Judicial District in southwestern Colorado.)

Kuenhold graduated from the University of Michigan Law School in 1969 and decided to apply his training to legal services after spending a summer in New York City working for the Mobilization Youth Legal Services. He joined VISTA, a domestic version of the Peace Corps.

"My commitment to do legal service work was tied to my feelings about the Vietnam War. I didn't believe in the war and VISTA and legal service work was my way to do service for my country. I wanted to do something positive rather than negative and this allowed me to do that." Judge Kuenhold's soft reassuring voice must sound non-threatening from the bench, even comforting.

He first heard of Skip Chase from Joseph Sax, his law school professor and a friend of Skip's. Professor Sax recommended Kuenhold look up Skip, who was starting a legal service program in rural Colorado. Kuenhold, who had enjoyed ski trips to Colorado, drove to the University of Colorado in Boulder, where Skip was teaching at the law school.

"I told him that I was a VISTA volunteer and I had also applied for a Reginald Heber Smith Community Lawyer Fellowship in poverty law and I wanted to work for the Rural Legal Services program. He got me assigned to the program." (Kuenhold got a letter of recommendation from Bill Prakken, a fellow Reggie.)

Skip hired Kuenhold to open CRLS's office in Alamosa (population hovering at 9,000), which serves as the county seat, the valley's legal, medical and retail hub and home of Adams State College, a four-year college with 2,500 resident students. Local legend has it that Alamosa ("cottonwood" in Spanish) went from a tent city in June, 1878 to a railroad center overnight when crews for the Denver & Rio Grande Railroad in Garland City, twenty miles to the east, put their mess hall on a railcar and hauled it to Alamosa to establish a new railhead.

Remembering the immediate impact Skip made, Judge Kuenhold said, "He was very charismatic. His enthusiasm affected everyone who wanted to work with him, including me. I wanted to recruit other attorneys and get them involved. He inspired me to work hard and go out and fight for people's rights and make the world better," Judge Kuenhold recalled, sitting in a conference room of the Alamosa County Courthouse, a brick two-story quasi-Mexican style building with a deep-set hacienda porch surrounding, on three sides, a grass courtyard with a non-functioning fountain in the center.

"Skip made you want to be the best you could be and to extend yourself for the benefit of others. If he was in the room, he was the focal point." Judge Kuenhold is a tall, handsome man, trim and relaxed, with a fondness for goats (of which he would like to raise a small herd someday, perhaps in retirement). "Skip could be loud, but mostly it was his presence. You wanted to hear what he had to say because it would be worth listening to."

In Alamosa, Kuenhold rented the first CRLS office rooms vacated by the county probation department, and called law school friends. "This is going to be a great deal. Come join me," he enthused. Within two years, the CRLS Alamosa staff grew to five attorneys and Kuenhold became the office manager.

Before Kuenhold could practice law in Alamosa, he had to go before the local bar association to be accredited. Back then, he wore a ponytail, blue jeans, and an open-collar work shirt, a style that reflected the attitude of other CRLS attorneys and of Skip. When he had to wear a coat-and-tie, the tie was most likely to be polka dot rather than a staid solid color or respectable strips. "I showed disdain for all the professional things the local bar association held dear. I rubbed it into their face. I eventually learned that was not a good approach. In the opinion of the local bar, I wasn't a real lawyer. There was a very heated debate that went on for several hours."

But, in the end, the local bar had no choice but to admit Kuenhold to practice law; he had a valid law degree and had passed the Colorado bar exam.

"Many of those who opposed me have since become friends. Now, as a judge, I dress more conservatively," he admitted.

"The very first time Skip and I came to Alamosa, we were sitting in the office of the Civil Rights Commission down the street from the courthouse," Judge Kuenhold recalled. "We were having a drink when someone came in to complain about the welfare department, something about a denied payment, I think. Skip immediately said, 'Let's go down to the welfare department.' We marched down there and met with the director, Leland McDaniels."

Skip could be a gentleman, very charming and diplomatic when he wanted, but this wasn't one of those times. Without knowing much about the particulars of the case, he aggressively got in McDaniels' face and accused the welfare department of violating all kinds of laws, although he couldn't cite which laws. For Skip, the technicalities of the law weren't the point. An injustice was being perpetuated, in his opinion, and should be addressed.

Jon Asher, who managed the CRLS Greeley office, described Skip's style as "ready, fire, aim."

"Some of us were a little more cautious in how we approached litigation of the legal rights of the poor," Asher said. "Skip thought I was a little too timid and too conservative in my approach, and I thought he was a little quick on the trigger. There is probably some truth in both."

Kuenhold later researched the case Skip forced his nose into; the welfare department was correct and the gung-ho idealistic lawyers totally off. "While we were wrong in that particular instance," Judge Kuenhold said, "Skip's ready, fire, aim attitude often produced good results. There were a lot of real things to shoot at."

With a client base of rural poor, CRLS's Alamosa office soon had a full work load of divorces, landlord/tenant disputes, wage issues, welfare cases, unemployment claims, often applying the state's *in forma pauperous* statute to waive filing fees for people who couldn't afford legal representation. Migrant farm workers were high on Skip's list of CRLS's priority clients and many of those cases involved housing and wages.

Recalling his days as a CRLS attorney, Judge Kuenhold said, "When I think of some of the hovels I visited. A farmer might rent

A barn west of Center, Colorado that has housed migrant farm workers.
Photo taken in 2010 by George Ron Waldie

out his housing to workers who didn't even work on his farm, so the incentive to fix those places up and make them nice was low."

For the farmer, decent migrant worker housing was an economic black hole. Proper housing with sanitation facilities would cost thousands of dollars in capital investment, and that investment would sit idle for eight months out of the year. The appreciation rate, increase of property taxes, utility fees and maintenance would eat up a good chunk of the average farmer's yearly profit. No wonder they tried to cut corners; converted chicken coops, haylofts with beds, slap-dash wood frame houses with outhouses were offered to migrants workers—who had little choice but to accept if they wanted the work.

"Back then, Bob Bowers, a county employee who worked for the local health department, had a great deal of sympathy for migrant workers and the conditions of the housing and health in their camps provided by the farmer," said Judge Kuenhold. "At the beginning of the harvest season, he'd take me around in his car and show a labor camp where the conditions were in violation of the law. That would get me pointed in the right direction. He was a very good man."

Payment of wages was also a frequent bone of contention between farmers and workers. The squeeze of money in/money out often had both groups tight-roping the fine line between profits and loss.

"I remember one case," Judge Kuenhold said. "The migrant workers had quit working because, due to a constant rain, they were not getting enough hours to support themselves. They wanted the pay due to them so they could go back to Texas and find more profitable work. It was the end of the season and this farmer said he wouldn't pay them until the coming Saturday. That meant the workers had to stay a whole week before they could leave."

From the farmer's point of view, the migrant workers were the hands needed to bring in the harvest. He had to keep them in place or lose his crop.

Going back to that day, Judge Kuenhold remembered, "I drove out to the farm in my blue VW van and jumped out. The farmer came out to greet me holding a shotgun. I had my doubts that it was a good idea coming out to the farm, but we ended up having a good conversation. I told him, 'Look, whatever else, the workers are going to be here for five days. They worked for you for three days and eight hours. You know how much you owe them and it's not much. I also know that this is inconvenient for you. But, as a human being, can't you cut the checks now so they can go home? If you were stranded and wanted to go home, wouldn't you hope that someone would do that for you?' I didn't get into a legal argument or threaten a lawsuit. I simply talked to him man-to-man. I was able to get the workers their checks. The farmer was a decent man."

CRLS attorneys sometimes found themselves in a conundrum when fighting for the rights of their clients. Take the case in Greeley labor camps. Skip had brought a suit against a sugar beet grower for providing substandard migrant worker housing that didn't meet state regulations. He won the case. The growers, who were not legally obliged to provide workers with housing, closed down the labor camps, forcing workers and their families to live in their cars or makeshift shelters.

"That taught me an important lesson," recalled Jon Asher, who was the CRLS office manager in Greeley. "Winning a case legally is not as important as working with your clients about what the ultimate outcome of litigation is likely to be, and is that going to result in a net gain to poor people. In that housing case, I don't think it played out the way Skip, or anybody else, hoped. It was pretty logical to expect that, rather than farmers incurring the additional cost of providing adequate housing, they were likely not going to provide housing at all. There was no way to force growers to provide housing.

"Skip brought all sorts of cases. Some were thoughtful and successful; many were thoughtful and not successful. He certainly thought it was better to sue people and lose than wait and sue them and win."

Judge Kuenhold, reflecting on Skip's approach, said, "There were times when Skip didn't care if he was technically legally right, and sometimes he should have cared when he didn't."

Like many good trial lawyers, Skip was always right even when he was wrong, according to Judge Kuenhold. Winning a case might not be the most important reason to go to trial; he would try a case to make a point of social justice or an inequity to start the discussion on the issue. He might not win that particular case but he'd set the stage for future cases to be brought on the same legal and social justice principles. Many civil rights lawyers employed the same tactic, often successfully.

Chapter 6

Them vs. Us

Skip's strategy to work hand-in-hand with the Colorado Migrant Council fostered a fundamental misunderstanding of CRLS that fueled much of the resentment against the organization. In the *Colorado Law Review* article relating his farm worker experience Skip wrote:

> *"It was my thought that a legal services program should work very closely with the Council, establishing offices in the same areas. The Council has imaginative, aggressive people on its staff that are making significant inroads in the areas of community organization and education. By establishing regular lines of communication with the Council, the legal services program would be educated as to the needs of the community it is to serve, have clients fed to it by Council employees working in the community, and, by an active part in the Council's adult education program, have the opportunity to appraise people in the community of their legal rights."*

As a result, CRLS became closely associated with the migrant worker community, an association that led to charges CRLS attorneys were "communists," "socialists," and "outside agitators." Farmers didn't want CRLS meddling in their affairs, stirring up trouble, giving the workers legal recourse to poor housing and unfair labor practices.

Moises Sandoval, an Alicia Patterson Foundation award winner and staff writer for *Maryknoll Magazine*, detailed cases of illegal conditions under which migrant workers lived and worked that still persisted in 1978 in his report "The Phantom Migrants."

"One such family is that of Gregorio Herrero (not his real name," Sandoval wrote. "In mid-January, he and his family were living in a small trailer alongside a barn on a farm near Windsor, Colo. The Herreros had no water, no inside plumbing and only a gas cook stove to heat the trailer. Herrero had worked only four hours the previous week at $2 an hour and the farmer had kept the $8 to apply to back rent for the trailer. Every member of the family—father, mother, and three small children—was sick. The only food was that brought by Migrant Council staffers. The farmer was charging Herreros $50 a month rent and $45 for electricity, although the Herreros had only a single light bulb and an ancient TV set. (The couple said the farmer had refused to show them the light bill.) The cost for gas was $75 for two months."

On a wage issue, Sandoval reported, "Migrant Council officials told of instances, especially in the northeast, where the contractors would negotiate $25 an acre for thinning the beets and then tell the workers that the grower paid only $15. The contractor would then keep $5 and the migrants would get $10."

Such conditions, which Skip learned first-hand from working with migrant families, spurred him to establish CRLS as a legal resource for migrant workers. The organization didn't advocate on social or political issues; CRLS lawyers took on cases brought to their attention. The proactive Colorado Migrant Council, which some farmers considered a thorn in their side, brought many cases to CRLS. VISTA volunteers active in setting up daycare for migrant workers' children, adult education classes and other socially orientated causes also brought cases to CRLS. And some CRLS lawyers, such as John

Kuenhold, were once VISTA volunteers. Many San Luis Valley farmers considered the CRLS, Colorado Migrant Council and VISTA as a triumvirate in collusion against the locals.

The prejudices and mood underlying the resentment against the Migrant Council, VISTA and CRLS came out in a letter written by Cecil W. Frutchey, a member of the Colorado Council on Migrant and Seasonal Agricultural Workers. In the letter, Frutchey resigned his Council membership because, in his opinion, "the Council is being used as a front to build a bureaucracy at the University [of Colorado] in Boulder and for very little else.

"From the beginning of the first VISTA program in the San Luis Valley, it is the opinion of many of us the general intent was to pit one segment of the population against the other, without any regard for the economy of the area or whether or not any realistic improvements could be brought about," he wrote.

Frutchey, a seed researcher from the Colorado State University in Fort Collins, worked in the San Luis Valley for years and lectured to nearly every VISTA group that came to the valley. In his resignation letter, he stated: "It was usually apparent, by their attitude, they [the volunteers] had been brain-washed before arrival. Young people, who only weeks before had never heard of the San Luis Valley, knew all of the reasons for the poverty. The farmers, the merchants, the County Commissioners, were the real rascals, oppressing the "poor" Spanish people. The wages were too low; there was no reason why the farmers could not pay more or provide better housing. No one asked if the price of potatoes, the price of sheep, or the price of cattle was too low.... It was obvious to those of us the VISTA and their supervisors had no intention of considering the rural-type economy of the San Luis Valley, or the problems involved in the cost-price squeeze of the farmers."

In his letter, Frutchey's statement on housing for migrant workers accurately reflected the sentiment of the valley's farmers: "The farmer is the only segment of industry expected to furnish housing for his employees. Then the government(s) tells him what type he has to build and what standards he has to meet. If the government wants special housing built for farm workers, it should build and maintain them. The farmer should not be required to make housing his responsibility. If society is concerned about the farm employee housing situation, then society should be responsible."

A class attitude of "haves" against "have-nots" was a familiar attitude, often rooted in racism, in the Valley. "There are many factors involved in poverty situations and anti-poverty action. Major among these are lack of ambition and industry.... In rural communities, schools and roads and hospitals are built by people who work hard and pay taxes, not by bureaucratic offices grinding out memos and important directives. In short, someone has to work to produce the needs of life, the food of life, and to meet the responsibilities of life. Poverty, generally, is due to a lack of responsibility of the poverty-stricken."

He acknowledged that the "Spanish people were here first. They had the first chance for the most lucrative land and the best water rights. They by-passed these opportunities. When they finally became aware of them, the Valley was growing into a prosperous agricultural area and the best land and water rights were no longer available. This left them but two alternatives: either to farm the poorer land or become farm workers. They have survived but generally have not prospered. Meanwhile, the development of the Valley has been largely due to the efforts of the farmers, business and professional people."

In conclusion, Frutchey wrote: "...let me say this is not meant to be a tirade against the Spanish people. They have contributed much to the San Luis Valley. They do 80% of the hard, menial work on the farms. The farmers need the farm workers. The farm workers also need the farmers. The farmers were providing the workers a living long before the OEO was a bureaucratic dream. Action to pit these segments against each other will gain little and lose much. The Spanish people have known many disadvantages. Some of these are inherent. Some are of their own making. Few are someone else's fault."

Against this backdrop, Skip and Bill Prakken pushed the CRLS into San Luis Valley.

CRLS played an influential role in the local community, according to Jennie Sanchez, a high profile activist in the San Luis Valley for more than forty years. "Skip Chase helped change the mentality of helplessness among the migrant workers and the poor in general. He had a great impact on the legal system in the Valley, there's not any doubt about that."

Sanchez, 79, born and raised in Center, Colorado, has lived in the small rural town all her life. A tiny, feisty woman with long gray hair and lovely brown eyes, Sanchez is a formidable organizing force in local politics and town issues, especially schools. Some see her as an outspoken hero willing to take on the power structure; others consider her a firebrand meddler.

"Here's an example of what I mean by Skip's influence empowering the local poor and disadvantaged," Sanchez said. "There was a local man who didn't speak very good English. He got in a fight and when he went to court the charges were read as 'assault and battery.' The man replied, 'I hit the guy but I sure in hell never stole any batteries.' Now, before Skip came to the valley and established CRLS, people who didn't speak or understand English, or were too poor to hire even a cheap lawyer, often pleaded guilty because they saw no other way out of their predicament. But the legal services program gave them an option. That's the difference today."

And, Sanchez pointed out, the presence of CRLS and the lifeline of hope it offered had personal and social consequences. "In understanding people who have been oppressed, you have another perspective on why people act like they do. Sometimes, the frustrated farm workers might want to kill their bosses because of working conditions or not getting full pay, but they don't. Instead, they beat up their wives or abuse their kids. But, with CRLS, they could apply their frustration and aggression to a court fight."

Sanchez first met Skip when she traveled to Boulder, where he was teaching at the University of Colorado Law School, to seek his help with a Center school issue.

"People were not happy about what was going on in our little town, our school district. In Center's school, it was not any different than in the segregated classrooms in the South. The town itself was segregated. *Mejicanos*[1] lived on the east side of Main Street and Anglos lived on the west side of town. *Mejicanos* could not buy a house on the west side of town. The town was divided. Every *mejicano* kid couldn't go to the normal first grade at age six because they were *mejicano* and couldn't speak English, which wasn't always true, as I'll explain. The teachers called this class the 'baby' class. That whole class was *mejicano*. They put my brother, who spoke English, in that class. He came home crying and told me what happened. I got him by the hand

---

1 *Mejicano* is the word Ms. Sanchez used to connote the Hispanic people in the Town of Center in the 1960s and earlier. They were descendants of the folks who had settled on land grants in what is now New Mexico. They became United States citizens when the U.S. border moved with the Treaty of Guadalupe Hidalgo. Center now has Mexican immigrants, "Mexicans." However, in the time period to which she referred, the Hispanic population were *mejicanos*.

and took him to the school district's superintendent's office, where I found other parents with the same complaint.

"That's the first time such people stood up for themselves. The superintendent transferred those families' kids into the regular classroom. The parents saw that they could do something about what was not right. But it was hits and misses. There wasn't anything we could hang on to. It wasn't until CRLS came that people felt strong enough to take on other issues."

Even when blatant segregation ended, the school used tracking to measure a student's ability. Many parents saw this as just another way to segregate the kids. That's when Sanchez traveled to Boulder and sought out Skip and asked him to file a lawsuit against the school district.

"He was overwhelmed with other issues and couldn't do it," Sanchez said. "But another CRLS lawyer, Mel Greenstein, got involved. We gained confidence that we could do more to fight for our rights. Here in Center, you can see how that has carried over. Several years later, we were able to get the Colorado Lawyer's Committee for Civil Rights to challenge the drawing of district lines for the Colorado General Assembly. The lawsuit used the Voting Rights Act. We were successful; it went all the way to the U.S. Supreme Court. We were able to draw a district that was fifty-one percent Hispanic so that we'd have the chance to get a Hispanic representative for House District 60, which is the district in which Center is located. Center would never have gotten to where it is without outside resources, like CRLS, helping."

Chapter 7

CRLS v. SEC. OF AGRICULTURE

In 1970, CRLS filed a class action lawsuit on behalf of migrant workers Gregorio Salazar and Lionel Sanchez and all other farm workers receiving less than their full wage as mandated by law. Skip and CRLS attorney Jean E. Dubofsky took the lead on behalf of sugar beet workers in northeastern Colorado versus the U.S. Secretary of Agriculture Clifford Hardin (Salazar v. Hardin: Cite as: 314 F. Supp. 1257).

The principle behind the lawsuit was the right to notice and due process before a person's property was seized due to debt. Sugar beet producers customarily paid one check to crew leaders who recruited and oversaw the workers. The crew leader then paid the individual migrant workers after deducting expenses he claimed owed him by the workers. In effect, the workers' property (wage) was being seized without due process or hearing, depriving the workers of the minimum wage they were entitled to receive. In contrast, if farm hands were local and not migrants, the farmer usually paid them by direct check with deductions, like social security, withheld. The CRLS lawsuit sought the same rights for the migrant workers.

The practice of paying the crew leader instead of the workers directly was upheld within Colorado law. However, Skip and Dubofsky contended that the state regulation 7 C.F.R. 862.15 was invalid because it was inconsistent with the federal regulation 7 U.S.C. 1131 (c) (1) that stated:

> That all persons employed on the farm in the production, cultivation, or harvesting of sugar beets or sugarcane with respect to which an application for payment is made shall have been paid in full for all such work, and shall have been paid wages therefore at rates not less than those that may be determined by the Secretary to be fair and reasonable after investigation and due notice and opportunity for public hearing....

The Sugar Act of 1948 provided the legal grounding for the case. Federal legislation subsidized the American sugar industry to keep prices artificially low as a barrier to foreign sugar growers, primarily in Cuba, from competing in the American market. In exchange, sugar producers were required to pay field workers wages determined to be fair and reasonable by the Secretary of Agriculture. (The sugar beet growers were, in 1973, required to pay at least $2.15 per hour or the piece rate.)

The CRLS case stated "issues in this case arise from the failure of the Secretary, in making his determination of fair and reasonable wages, to accept the demands made by representatives of the workers." The demands included that workers be paid directly by the producer in such a form (for example a check) that was accountable. The lawsuit contended that the Secretary of Agriculture acted arbitrarily and capriciously in not exercising that responsibility.

Chase and Dubofsky demanded a permanent injunction against the Secretary of Agriculture, prohibiting sugar subsidies to any person who paid crew leaders rather than sugar beet workers directly. The government's counter-argument was that the Secretary of Agriculture was only legally bound to set the minimum wage and not to determine or supervise the method of payment.

According to CRLS, nothing in the Colorado regulation suggested "…that diminished worker compensation is to be tolerated. It is also clear that under the terms of the statutory condition set forth in 1131 (c) (1), the burden of carrying out this Congressional intent is cast upon each individual producer."

According to the statute, a producer of sugar beets shall be deemed to have complied with the wage provisions of the act [Sugar Act of 1948] if all persons employed on the farm in production, cultivation, or harvesting of sugar beets as provided in 863.12 has been paid in accordance with the following:

> If a producer employs workers through a labor contractor or crew leader and makes payment of workers' wages to him, the producer shall obtain from such contractor or crew leader (a) a copy of his authorization signed by each worker to collect wages due each such worker; (b) a wage record sheet showing the amounts earned and due each worker; and (c) a written representation that he will pay to each worker the wage rates agreed by the contractor and the producer but in an event less than those provided by this part.

Chase and Dubofsky argued "Congress intended to place ultimate responsibility for insuring full payment to workers on the producer, and therefore that 7 C.F.R. 862.15 conflicts with this intent in that it allows the producer to evade the statutorily imposed responsibility."

United States Court Judge William E. Doyle ruled in favor of CRLS, holding the Colorado regulation void and invalid as "inconsistent with and in direct contravention of 7 U.S.C. 1131 (c) (1)." The decision stated that the Secretary of Agriculture is "permanently enjoined from making sugar payments to any Colorado sugar beet producer who after the date of this order pays wages due to farm workers to a crew leader or labor contractor."

CRLS won a clear and decisive victory.

The government appealed the case to the United States Court of Appeals, Tenth Circuit. In the 1973 decision, the appeals court overturned the original ruling on the grounds that the CRLS's arguments "have strayed from the narrow question of whether the Secretary, in the exercise of is rulemaking powers, acted arbitrarily or capriciously." The ruling stated "the Secretary made it clear that the workers' proposals were rejected not only because they were not authorized by the Sugar Act, but also that they (the workers' proposals) were deemed to be impractical and undesirable...."

In a similar case, CRLS filed suit in federal court accusing the Colorado Department of Welfare of applying the federal food stamp regulations in a manner discriminatory to migrant farm workers. Food stamps, sold on the basis of family income, were issued to migrant farm workers on an anticipated income. The migrants often wound up paying an unreasonably high price or were denied stamps altogether. The lawsuit asked for a refund of alleged overcharges to migrant families and for formulation of new regulations by the U.S. Secretary of Agriculture.

In the midst of the sugar beet case, Skip found another of his "ready, fire, aim" spontaneous causes—Tep Falcon. He noticed her during a testimony hearing, where she told of her experience with the migrant workers in Fort Lupton regarding food stamps, wages and housing issues. She sat slumped at the table in the hearing room, obviously upset. When inquiring, 'What's wrong?' Skip got an earful.

At the time, Tep was a CU student and, although an Anglo, was deeply involved in the United Mexican-American Student organization (she married the Chicano activist Ricardo Falcon) and worked for the Migrant Council. As an outspoken and fiery speaker on farm worker issues on and off campus, she earned a reputation as an agitator. When noticed by Skip, she was fuming from being turned down for a job at the CU registrar's office because of her activism.

Skip's immediate response: "Let's sue them," meaning his employer, the University of Colorado, and the State of Colorado.

"I told him, 'We can't sue them'," Tep recalled at her home in Denver. "He said, 'Yes, we can.' I said, 'It's against my religion. I'm Catholic.' He said, 'Are you crazy? If they did this to you, what do you think they're doing to other people?' So he convinced me to sue the University."

The first step was to arrange a meeting with the woman who refused Tep the job, Betty Lewis, along with several CU department deans and Tep's father, an attorney. Lewis, a former Marine, confirmed that she knew what was good for the University of Colorado and the United States of America and that Tep and her kind were not it.

"She said that I would not get a job in her office," Tep said. "The civil rights stuff was everywhere so who in their right mind would say something like that?"

At the meeting, the university representatives asked Tep what she wanted.

"I want to be paid," she replied.

"But we can't pay you for work you haven't done, since you were never hired," the University representatives reasoned.

"Then Lewis should pay me," Tep shot back. "Open up her wallet and pay me. She's the one who deprived me of income."

The University officials didn't think that was correct either. They agreed to put a reprimand in Lewis's file, suggesting that the procedure would be a victory for Tep.

Tep had another suggestion: She and Lewis step outside and physically fight, fisticuffs, hair pulling, and wrestling, whatever it took to determine a clear winner. "The university people said to my father, 'Mr. Tepley, is this a joke?' He replied, 'I don't think so. She's serious.'"

"I'm not a good fighter," Tep admitted. "Lewis was older, bigger and had been a Marine. If I'm laying down in the gutter, then I know I lost. If she is laying down in the gutter, then I know I've won."

The University turned down her offer. She'd have to settle for a reprimand in Lewis's file.

Some weeks later, Tep learned that a reprimand had never been issued. She was steamed, fighting mad. The University had lied to her, treated her with disrespect, tossed her complaint aside. That's when Skip noticed her sitting next to him at the sugar beet hearing table and asked, "What's your problem?" And the fight was on.

The case never went to court, but Skip did present her with a settlement check. "I'm pretty sure it was from the University," Tep said casting her memory back nearly forty years. "My mind sometimes tells me, 'Was it from Skip?' My mother wanted me to give the money, about $600 I think, back to the University to buy turf for the football field. She was a big CU football fan. I gave it to the United Farm Workers instead."

Chapter 8

Enemies Attack CRLS

By 1972, four years after it's founding, CRLS had a presence in nineteen Colorado counties and brought numerous lawsuits on behalf of migrant workers and the rural poor. The legal work attracted enemies. A political attack was orchestrated to gut CRLS and curtail its influence.

Rural small town officials complained of CRLS representation of the poor, who sought help in organizing labor unions, contesting school dress codes, and airing grievances about their economic distress. Such activism had "split the community."

Colorado Farm Bureau charged that CRLS attorneys harassed farmers with lawsuits seeking to enforce regulations regarding substandard housing for migrant workers and the employment of illegal aliens from Mexico.

CRLS lawyers did take farmers to court for alleged violations of the State Health Department regulation prohibiting substandard housing for migrant farm workers and for alleged violations of federal statutes prohibiting the employment of illegal aliens from Mexico.

In response to the complaints, CRLS stated, "The silence of racial and economic minorities in the past has undoubtedly been mistaken by some as acceptance of the conditions of life in rural Colorado. Disputes and conflicts that may have been hidden beneath the surface for years because poor persons were unable to present their positions effectively without legal representation or were unaware of their rights have now come out in the open and are receiving attention.

"There is no basis for concluding that CRLS employees have deliberately caused controversies, and it is irresponsible for the task force members to characterize the efforts of CRLS personnel as causing 'polarization' in the communities where they work."

That statement didn't mollify the forces aligned against CRLS. The Colorado Farm Bureau took a leading role in organizing allied forces to gut the legal service organization. One such attempt was a petition drive calling for Colorado Governor John Love to "stem the intolerable harassment of Colorado's farmers and ranchers by Colorado Rural Legal Services." The Farm Bureau purported CRLS was "requiring farmers and ranchers and other taxpaying citizens to become involved in costly legal actions."

The Rural Chamber of Commerce complained that farmers "have enough troubles with nature to produce a living and don't need CRLS to make it rougher. The farmer and producer represent about 18 to 20 million dollars in this area; we need to protect them." Farmers feel "it's unfair to use our own tax money to fight us."

Farm Bureau leaders, accompanied by five state representatives from rural counties, delivered 205 petitions with signatures of 6,929 farmers and ranchers to the governor. They demanded that the governor rescind the agreement under which the federal Office of Equal Opportunity funneled $489,000 annually in federal money to CRLS through the governor's office.

Dean Kittle, administrative officer of the Farm Bureau, stated, "Colorado Rural Legal Service is working on broad legal issues on a very narrow legal basis."

In the Farm Bureau report to the governor, Grand Junction Chamber of Commerce member Jack Williams stated CRLS lawsuits are "unjust" and "merely to harass." An unidentified Mesa County commissioner stated, "They (CRLS) literally harass us, and further, they sue us to make us comply with rules that we don't have money to comply with." La Junta mayor Keith Webb reportedly noted that CRLS "did engage in suits that are bad for (their) image."

A 32-page report compiled by the task force appointed by Governor Love was critical of the CRLS. The report contained interviews with more than seventy farmers, local officials, merchants, lawyers and others in rural agricultural communities surrounding Grand Junction and in the San Luis Valley, the Arkansas Valley and northern Colorado. Interviews with rural poor whom CRLS served or with the county and district court judges before whom the CRLS lawyers practiced were not included in the report.

The report bristled with inaccuracies, hearsay, unsubstantiated generalities, distortions and undisguised displays of bias, according to press investigations. The report contained no evidence to document the truth of the charges made or details of claims of lawsuit harassment because of "attorney-client privilege," according to stories in Denver's major newspapers.

Yet, the governor's task force recommended that Governor Love transform CRLS into a quasi-public agency to "ensure that proper supervision is given to the total program…and that CRLS be broken into four regional areas under the control of local advisory groups."

The recommendation would essentially gut the CRLS. The legal service would lose its autonomy and be under the thumb of "local advisory groups" conceivably made up of the people who opposed CRLS.

Jesse Manzanares, then acting chairman of the CRLS board of directors, cautioned in a memo to staffers, clients and friends of CRLS "that serious effort and campaign is being waged by the State

Office of Economic Opportunity to take over the role and function of CRLS." The state OEO office, which reports to the governor's office, functions as a monitor for dozens of federally funded OEO programs in Colorado.

Manzarares wrote that the state OEO office "has prepared and submitted to the Governor a proposal to set up an entirely new program which would essentially take over the CRLS program." This move was "in apparent response to the recent task force investigation conducted by Jake R. Valdez, former state OEO director, John R. Lopez, deputy director for the state OEO, and James K. Kreutz, assistant attorney general for the state of Colorado."

In his memo, Manzanares stated that the OEO proposal was "an extremely poor, if not disastrous substitute for CRLS. Its basic organization and structure radiate the total lack of any sensitivity or understanding of poor people and of legal services to rural poor people."

Actually, Manzanares was more sanguine than his dire warnings sounded. "I knew Jake Valdez, who was from San Luis Valley and a pretty good guy," Manzanares recalled. "We talked about it and I came away thinking that there was a lot of pressure being put on the governor to try and kill the CRLS funding. But Jake told me it wasn't going to happen. Governor Love was not a real conservative redneck guy. He was a moderate Republican, for the lack of a better word. He never took seriously the efforts of the growers to destroy CRLS."

Governor Love initially refused to approve more than the first ninety days of the CRLS fiscal budget, apparently on the basis of the report. Under federal regulations, the budget could have taken effect without the governor's signature.

After discussions with the governor, CRLS staffers agreed that cases of the rural poor as a group would be filed only after consultation with the CRLS research team and administrators at the Denver office.

"We, Skip and myself and others from CRLS, were summoned to the governor's office," recalled Bill Prakken. "The opposition to CRLS wanted the governor to put a slow-down on our program. They objected to what they thought was CRLS going out and generating cases and looking for plaintiffs, rather than plaintiffs coming to us with some grievance. We met with Governor Love and I don't think he was interested in shutting us down. He wanted to get to the bottom of the issues of the growers and the Farm Bureau."

In the end, Governor Love did not implement the task force's proposals and CRLS received its full funding.

Chapter 9

Coup against Skip

The year 1972 was pivotal for CRLS and for Skip. The organization was fighting off its critics and internal strife. Skip faced personal battles. Within CRLS, Chicano militants agitated to take control of CRLS and demanded that Skip be replaced with a Chicano.

"It was a painful period of time," Bill Prakken said of the clash. "A lot of the guys demanding Skip resign or be fired were Chicano activists who didn't feel the program had a strong enough Chicano orientation. The rest of us on the staff didn't share that feeling."

A small group of young Chicano activists, most not connected to the CU law school, physically took over the CRLS office. Skip and the staff moved to another room down the hall. Prakken shuttled back and forth conveying messages and terms.

"He was accused of things that were just not so, like he was not a friend of the Chicanos, that he wasn't brown enough, that sort of thing," Prakken said, still unhappy about the move against Skip forty years after the event.

Rose-Avila, Skip's first Chicano CRLS hire and personal friend, offered an explanation for the takeover:

"The Chicano Power crusade really got going in 1968-69. We were embroiled and caught up by the emotions of the world. Martin Luther King had been assassinated, Bobby Kennedy killed, the Olympics with Tommy Smith and Juan Carlos raising their clinched fists on the winner's podium. That stuff was in the air, a lot of excitement about letting the people take over.

"Part of the Chicano movement from 1969 on we needed to be culturally fixed with the programs that were supposed to serve the Latino community. We felt Latinos/Chicanos should run the programs. So there was a lot of push on a lot of programs across the state and nationally to get the people targeted for help to have a role in running the programs. A great number of the cases CRLS took on were farm worker cases and most of the workers were Chicano. They were the most identifiable clients of CRLS. Admittedly, CRLS did a lot of sexual abuse, divorce and welfare cases, and most of the people on welfare were white. But the Chicanos felt CRLS was the one legal program they could take over and make an impact. Chicanos went through a process of trying to take over everything serving us. You pick your targets. Where do you think you have an impact? That's why they took it over."

To that end, some within the Chicano movement, especially those associated with the more militant political elements, moved to force out Skip as CRLS director. A successful effort was also made to remove Howard Higman as head of the Colorado Migrant Council and replace him, and Anglo board members, with Chicanos.

Recalling that time, Rose-Avila said, "I was in Center, Colorado, working as a community/migrant worker organizer for the United Farm Workers. I had heard on the grapevine that these guys—I believed it was Ray Otero, Freddy Granados, Ediberto Teran and Raymundo 'Tigre' Perez—were planning to physically take over the CRLS office in the old crumbling St. Gertrude building. Tigre called me, as we were tight, and said they were going to ask Skip Chase to step down. It was time for a Chicano to be the CRLS director. 'Where do you stand on this?' he demanded. 'Shouldn't you support us in getting rid

Coup Against Skip

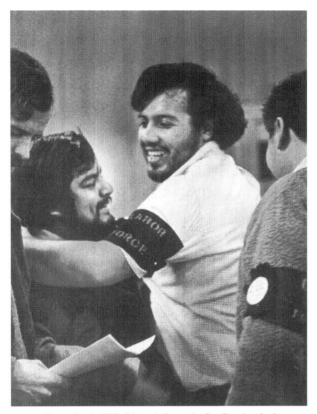

Photo taken in 1970 of the end of a ten-day fast. Prominently shown are Len Rose-Avila (wearing arm band), who worked for CRLS, and Raymundo 'Tigre' Perez (second from left), one of the Chicano activists who took over the CRLS office, which led to Skip Chase's resignation. Denver Public Library Western History Collection, Z-827

of Skip? We need you because you're a farm worker leader. You'll be the icing on the cake. You would lend us a lot of credibility because you worked for CRLS as a community coordinator and you worked for the Migrant Council. You've been asking for Latinos/Chicanos to take over leadership positions. How could you be opposed?'

"They told me they were planning to hold a press conference to announce that Skip had to be fired. I was given a lot of ammunition about how Chicanos should take over Skip's position. In that there was some vague reason about Jewishness. Skip was a little Jewish.

113

"I was taken back. I loved Skip and he was good to me. Then they started giving me contextual stuff and pushing me to join them at the press conference. We talked about 30-45 minutes about Chicano politics and why Skip should step down so a Latino could do the job. I'm not feeling right about this but finally I said, 'Yeah, I think a Chicano should have the job. I'll come to Boulder for the press conference and say that I want Skip to step down but on one condition, I be allowed to talk about all that Skip did. I have to talk about how he defended people when he was not paid, when he stood up for us, when he had this mission, when he took on cases that jeopardized his professorship. When he had the vision to go out and get attorneys and train them and to hire me.'

"I told them, 'If you let me say who Skip is then I can ask for his resignation. You've got to say that he was with the struggle before you guys decided you were Chicanos. You've got to say the fact that there is nothing wrong with Skip or his leadership. It's just that our time has come. And if you can't say the history, we can't ask for him to leave. You have to allow to me say all those things before I'd asked him to resign. I have to say who the man was and what he contributed. If you do not allow me to do that, I cannot go after him.'

"They told me, 'You've sold out to a white man.' And I said, 'Best person I've sold out to today. I'm not going to show up if you can't say who the man really is.'"

Rose-Avila didn't attend the press conference.

As the crisis between the activists and Skip dragged on, Bill Prakken returned to Trinidad, in southern Colorado, where he ran the CRLS office. As co-founder of CRLS, he was not asked to resign.

Jesse Manzanares, one of five attorneys licensed in Colorado at the time, was asked to become the acting chair of the CLRS board to mediate the crisis. "The kids were raising hell because no Hispanics were involved in the CRLS big picture," Manzanares said from his law office in Trinidad, Colorado. "I got involved, basically, to come to the defense of Skip and try to calm things down."

At the time Manzanares was dean at the University of Denver charged with recruiting more Hispanics into the law program. "What upset the kids was that no Hispanics were involved in the leadership of CRLS initially," he said. "There was a lot of money flowing from the federal government through of the Office of Economic Opportunity. The perception of the people involved in the takeover was that you can go get some of that money, and a lot of people did, and you could spend it to hire folks. But since there were no Hispanics in leadership roles, they didn't have that power. These kids believed that since they were working with migrant laborers, everyone in the program should be Hispanic. Of course, that's unrealistic. Nevertheless, some of those kids thought they ought to be controlling the money and hiring their own people. That was pretty short sighted and stupid, but that's what they thought."

The negotiations dragged on without any real resolution. Tempers flared. People slammed doors; racism more than reason colored the situation. The emotionally charged youth were fighting for an ideology and practical power. Skip and his supporters sought to keep experienced people in place to oversee the program. The conflict was a clash of cultures, of mind-sets, of the oppressed pushing to the front to take their share and of those who had created the program battling to keep it intact.

"It was tumultuous, very unpleasant, very difficult, a very racially divisive period," stated Jon Asher, then a CRLS attorney. "Skip did not handle the situation artfully, shall we say. He thought he could just beat up the opposition as opposed to really trying to deal with it. He put up a spirited defense and this strung out over a period of time.

The issue was, who owns a program? Was it Skip because he started it? Or was it the client community and the Hispanic community who were the primary beneficiaries of the program? Most of the CRLS clients were white but, nevertheless, it was seen as a heavily migrant Hispanic program. I don't think the data ever showed that the majority of the clients were Hispanic. Skip did a great job of recruiting and encouraging and supporting Hispanic/Latino lawyers who didn't want a white director. A group of people who were very close to Skip left CRLS around that time."

Finally, Skip agreed to step aside, and his assistant, Daniel M. Holguin, was appointed acting head until the board hired a permanent replacement. Jack Lang, administrative coordinator of CRLS Boulder headquarters at the time, said Skip's decision was in keeping with a "standing commitment"—both on his part and that of CRLS—to put a Chicano in charge as soon as possible. According to Lang, Skip had planned to resign the following May and return to the faculty of the University of Colorado Law School.

According to family and friends, Skip was devastated by his removal. CRLS was his baby, the manifested expression of his idealism and belief in the purpose of law. Equal rights and protection under the law was the cornerstone of his career. He had worked in the fields with migrant workers and shared their housing conditions. He had applied his years of training in law to bring them justice, even put his academic career on hold to establish CRLS. He had rushed the ramparts of prejudice and racism and injustice for their cause, a legal brief held high as a battleground pennant. And they spurned him. They rejected him. That was hard for Skip to swallow.

Yet, he never ranted or raved about the injustice done to him. Whatever bitterness he may have felt was never uttered, at least not in public. His natural competitive instinct to use his metaphorically strong wrestler's neck to resist defeat may have kicked in, but he reined it back. By philosophically agreeing to honor the Chicanos' demands in the best interest of their cause, Skip accepted his individual defeat to give the team a victory.

Bill Prakken had a more prosaic explanation: "I think he just got tired of it all, said to hell with it, I'm not going to put up with this, and resigned. His wife Nancy called me and chewed me out because I didn't come to Skip's defense. She let me know in no uncertain terms that I should have been more aggressive in his defense. It was a very, very painful time."

In assessing CRLS after Skip was forced out, Rose-Avila said, "To be honest, there were good people who came in after Skip and did great legislation. But Skip had an aura about him. I never felt that from any director who came after him. He was the spiritual leader and risk taker. Everyone who works in the legal services programs is a risk taker but none like Skip."

Chapter 10

Life after CRLS

After the coup that ousted him from CRLS, Skip devoted his time to teaching and litigating cases on equal protection and civil rights. His courses on Constitutional law, contracts and equal protection under the law were demanding not only because of the classroom work but also because he made students think about the law as a personal mission. He taught that lawyers are not neutral. Lawyers are first and foremost people guided by values and moved by a passion to make things right.

Don Miller, an attorney who credits Skip's strong influence on his law career, said, "Skip's lesson was that the law could be used as an instrument to bring about justice and equality for those who had been denied justice and equality in our society. There is value in the commitment to fight the good fight. Even if you lose, we as a people, we as a society, are better for the effort. Skip stood up for values and principles that weren't always the most popular at the time. Perhaps more importantly, this world is a better place because he inspired others to carry on in the tradition."

One lesson Miller learned working with Skip: "As a lawyer, if you wait until you're comfortable with all the procedures and legal theories and technical skills, you won't ever get anything done. When Skip saw an injustice, we were going to do something about it. We were going to sue the bastards! And we were going to do it now! It was a lesson in effectiveness and getting the job done."

Life After CRLS

View of the Fleming Law Building at the University of Colorado where Skip Chase taught. Photo taken in 2010 by George Ron Waldie

Skip loved to teach and did so with excitement and contagious enthusiasm that lit a fire in students to serve others and to find intellectual stimulus in the law. He knew the law cases he taught like old friends and brought that affection and familiarity into the classroom. His classroom work earned him nominations to the Board of Governors of the Society of American Law Teachers (SALT), a community of progressive law teachers working for justice and diversity.

In the classroom he wore blue jeans, a work shirt and necklaces of coral or turquoise or Navajo squash blossom design. This style of informal personal warmth didn't diminish the respect he commanded. In the classroom, as well as in the courtroom, he spoke as a lawyer, was incredibly articulate and did his research. But he was not beyond doing, with another faculty member, a song and dance routine of Gilbert and Sullivan's "Trial by Jury" as an introduction to law for students. He loved putting his heart into having fun with people.

"Skip was beloved by his students," according to David Getches. "He inspired his students to be activists. Some of his students participated in civil rights demonstrations, which was disconcerting to his dean, Courtland Peterson. Skip was luring the students to his camp, while the dean was trying to run a program, keep students attending class and such."

Skip may have been a beloved and inspirational teacher, but Bill Prakken put that in perspective. "Skip was not the greatest professor that came down the pike, which is kind of surprising because he had a lot of energy. I would have thought he'd be great at teaching. He inspired a lot of students, but I got the sense that it wasn't because he was great in the classroom but because of his personality."

Skip received mixed reviews from his students. Some regarded him as a superb teacher; others, such as Susan Corle, nee McGee, now an attorney, remembered him as a poor teacher. "I had Skip Chase as a Con Law professor at CU. I didn't think he was a good professor. He was way wrapped up in his own war stories. I don't think he did a very good job teaching us Con Law. I came out of there not really knowing a lot about Con Law. I can't even say there was a particular part of the Constitution he focused on. My husband was in the law school at the same time and we had the class together. We were just dating at the time. His memory is that he stopped going to the class after two sessions because he figured he'd learn it from the book. He was not at all happy with the way Skip taught.

"Skip had a lot of energy and a lot of passion about what he was talking about, but it was so much his war stories, the cases he had been involved with. The war stories were connected to the Constitution but it was so scattered and disorganized you didn't get a feel for, OK, I'm going to start with Article One, then go to Article Two. It wasn't presented in any organized fashion where you could get a grip on the

Constitution, which is what you're supposed to come of a class like that with, an overall grip of what the whole document means and does."

Besides teaching, Skip continued to be active in the courts. The rights of individuals and championing the little guy was the binding thread in his legal work and philosophy, as his published cases show:

– a lawsuit to admit a fellow attorney to the bar despite his conviction of a felony (possession of marijuana).

– the challenge of an employee's discharge for an alleged role in an unauthorized and illegal work stoppage.

– the termination of food service workers for failing to comply with the "no-beard" rule.

– a class action challenging the placement of inmates in punitive and administrative segregation alleging violations of due process.

– a claim by pretrial detainees in county jail stating that they had been denied a constitutional right to a program for contact visitation.

– the challenge, by a high school student, of the constitutionality of high school transfer procedures where officials did not provide for a hearing.

– the challenge, by a student, of the Colorado statute which prevents students at state universities from receiving in-state tuition until they have lived in the state for one year.

– the challenge of a decision denying unemployment compensation.

– the issuance of a temporary restraining order enjoining defendants from using force, threats, or intimidation to prevent the growing and harvesting of lettuce.

– a constitutional challenge to Colorado statutes that deny aliens the right to vote in school elections.

Skip also signed his name in support of the GI Civil Liberties Defense Committee, which, during the Vietnam War, took cases to defend soldiers' civil rights for speaking out against the war. (The long list of names in support included Noam Chomsky and James Baldwin and the committee's honorary chairman Lord Bertrand Russell.)

The Ft. Hood Three exemplified the type of case taken on by the defense committee. On July 7, 1966, federal agents abducted three soldiers stationed at Ft. Hood on their way to speak out at a public anti-war meeting at the Community Church. In a statement, the soldiers, Pfc. James Johnson, Pvt. David Samas and Pvt. Dennis Mora 142 Signal Battalion, 2nd Armored Division, said "We have decided to take a stand against this war, which we consider immoral, illegal and unjust.... We intend to report as ordered to the Oakland Army Terminal, but under no circumstances will we board ship for Vietnam. We are prepared to face Court Martial if necessary."

The soldiers were arrested and charged with violating Article 134 of the UCMJ (Article 134 is considered a "catch-all" that encompasses offenses not specifically listed in the Manual for Court-Martial. UCMJ stands for Uniform Code of Military Justice.) Despite support from the GI Civil Liberties Defense Committee, the three soldiers were court-martialed at Ft. Dix on September 7-9, 1966 and found guilty. Samas and Mora were sentenced to three years hard labor and Johnson to five years hard labor. Pete Seeger wrote the ballad "The Ft. Hood Three" commemorating the three anti-war protest soldiers.

In 1979, Skip, as American Civil Liberties Union attorney on behalf of Citizens Concerned for Separation of Church and State, sued Denver City and County to prevent the "displaying, storing, and appropriating public funds for the nativity scene (crèche) in front of and within the City and County Building."

The Christmas Lighting Program, which included Santa Claus, an elves' toy shop, reindeer and other Christmas trappings, had been produced with taxpayers' money annually for eight years. The suit requested the removal of the nativity scene from the display because of the use of taxpayers' money was a violation of the First (freedom of speech) and Fourteenth (citizenship rights not to be abridged) Amendments to the United States Constitution.

Skip won the case. On December 17, the court ruled that the nativity scene "is a religious symbol and that by including it in the Christmas display the City and County of Denver violated the Fourteenth Amendment to the United States Constitution." The judge ordered the display removed within forty-eight hours.

The next day the City and County appealed the decision to the United States Court of Appeals, Tenth District to stay the enforcement of the district court's ruling. A stay was granted the same day. Skip et al countered by filing a "Petition for Rehearing and a Suggestion for Rehearing en Banc," which was denied by the appeals court on December 28. Two days later, Skip applied to the United States Supreme Court to vacate the stay order.

Nearly a month later, January 21, 1980, the U.S. Supreme Court denied the application on the ground that the court was "without jurisdiction over this cause on appeal, we cannot reach the merits of the dispute involving the alleged violation of the Establishment Clause of the First Amendment to the United States Constitution by reason of the Nativity Scene display." The appeal was dismissed and remanded back to the district court with instruction to vacate the stay judgment for want of jurisdiction.

Skip, assisted by Dan Israel, appealed the decision. "We made the standard First Amendment arguments and some not so standard," Israel said. "One argument we showcased was particularly important to Skip: the city's display of a Nativity scene sent a message that the City and County of Denver building was a place for Christians. Skip's particular concern was how the message was being felt by non-Christian school children. That concern captured a lot of what Skip was about. Government and the benefits of society should be shared. Every effort should be made to include people, not exclude them. The doctrine of separation of Church and State was more than a religious issue. It implicated basic human rights. That theme guided a lot of Skip's thinking. It counted for his view of civil rights and equal protection."

The United States Court of Appeals, in a September 4, 1980 decision, dismissed the appeal and remanded the case to the District Court with instruction to vacate the judgment of December 17, 1979, for want of jurisdiction.

According to Bill Cohen, an original CRLS board member, "The symbol of Christianity on public land gave the impression that the government was endorsing that religion. Skip was concerned that kids of other faiths, especially Jewish kids, would feel like outsiders when looking up and seeing that lighted star during the holiday season (as displayed on a mountain outside Boulder), that they might feel second class. Skip was very sensitive to the prohibition of any appearance of an established state religion. Even in the 1820s, many of the northeast states in our country had official state religions, despite the Constitution ban on such a practice. The echo of the Inquisition, when in the Middle Ages many Jews were burned at the stake for their religious beliefs or falsely converted to Christianity to avoid such a fate, is still heard in the Jewish consciousness."

In 1981, Skip again tried to appeal the Citizens Concerned for Separation of Church and State v. City & County of Denver, and again was turned down by the court, citing the previous ruling.

The nativity scene remains part of the city-sponsored display in central Denver despite protests, the latest one held in December 2010.

Skip brought a similar lawsuit against the City of Boulder for its support of a holiday lighted star on the side of the mountain overlooking the town. He was not successful with that litigation, either.

The nativity scene suit was one of nearly twenty cases Skip took to court while on the payroll of the CU Law School. (He filed four cases and three appeals while on leave from his teaching duties to organize CRLS). In one case, Skip sued his employer, the University of Colorado, on behalf of food service workers fired for refusing to shave off their beards (Chiappe v. State Personnel Board, 1981). He lost that case. The court ruled that the University did not act arbitrarily in enforcing the no beard rule and in making it a condition of employment. The appointing authority, in this case the University, was entitled to a presumption of regularity, in the court's opinion, and that the liberty interest in selecting one's appearance is much less significant than other constitutional liberties.

In the Gurule v. Wilson case (1981), Skip was challenged for listing the law school facilities as an overhead expense, which he passed on to the clients. The court held that the expense was proper and awarded Skip $6,007.50 for his legal services.

Skip's legal activism didn't endear him to the then Dean of CU Law School Courtland Peterson. "Skip was certainly an activist member of the faculty and that put him at odds with his dean," according to David Getches. "At one point, Skip was picketing a liquor store because they were selling Gallo wine. (This was in support of the California grape picker's boycott.) He was constantly getting crossways with Court Peterson. Skip did not make it easy for Court."

In one case, Skip tried to sue the City of Boulder over prisoners in the city jail not being provided the type of organic food they requested. That case also failed and was seen by some as frivolous.

The seeming contraction of Skip's intellectual ardor for the law and his willingness to take on seemingly trivial cases earned him sideway glances from some of his faculty colleagues, particularly his more conservative peers. Bob Nagel, a nationally recognized Constitutional law scholar who occupies the only endowed chair at the CU Law School, recalled an incident that begged askance from some of the "old school" faculty. Skip took a year sabbatical, a time most academics devote to research and writing. Skip rode his bike across Canada. Instead of producing a scholarly book, he wrote a memoir of the trip.

"I'd go back to the secretaries to give them work and I'd ask what they were working on," Nagel recalled. "They'd say, 'I'm typing Skip's travel log.' But Skip had academic and intellectual interests that are underestimated because of his public persona."

Nagel first met Skip in 1971 when, as a second-year Yale law student, he worked a summer for CRLS in the San Luis Valley.

"In one case, I was trying to reinstate a land grant case," Professor Nagel recalled in his office at the CU Law School. "Some of the Hispanics claimed to have interest in the Sangre de Cristo range there. The case had been in litigation for years and years and plaintiffs had pretty much lost. CRLS was interested in finding some way to revive the litigation. It was fashionable at that time to bring cases challenging the way migrant workers were kept fairly isolated on those ranches. We were trying to get right of access to the workers involved in the land grant case. A bunch of us law students went out to the ranch and got kicked off."

Life After CRLS

After practicing law for three and half years, Nagel decided he wanted to teach law. He wrote to Skip seeking advice. Skip advised him of an opening at the CU Law School and urged him to come to Boulder and interview.

"When I came out, he took me on a hike before we went to his house. The custom in those days was before the interview you met the faculty in someone's house for a drink and chat. Skip shepherded me through that. He was very cordial, very pleasant, but he had to keep a distance from me because, as he explained, a lot of people would distrust anybody he was supporting. He didn't want to appear to be too much of a booster for me because it would hurt me when the faculty voted."

Skip had a different style than the other professors. He wore blue jeans and beads to class; they wore jackets and ties. He took the law and his students out of the classroom; they delivered the more traditional lectures where the students sat and took notes. Skip was an activist; they taught. He was one-of-a-kind within the law school and the bird with the brightest feathers invites judgment by the rest of the flock.

"I'm sure some of the faculty thought he wasn't academic enough, didn't do enough academic work," Nagel said. "They also thought he was spending too much time litigating these public interest cases. Some had specific objections and thought he shouldn't be spending so much time on them. But he was well liked. Even people who disapproved of some of the things he did thought he was a very nice guy."

At that time, 1975, a cultural change was happening within the CU Law School, as exemplified by the hiring of Bob Nagel and Bill Pizzi. Until then, being published in esteemed law reviews was not a high demand placed on CU law professors by the administration. But Nagel and Pizzi were hired with specific instructions to publish articles in top-rank law reviews. (They subsequently published in the *Stanford Law Review* and the *University of Chicago Law Review* respectively.) The university's administration wanted to burnish the law school's image.

"The old school model for legal education prior to the mid-1970s dominated the school," according to Nagel. "A lot of the faculty either didn't do scholarship, or they did a different kind of scholarship than we do now. A lot of professors thought teaching was their main function along with consulting, keeping up ties with the local bar association and public service. For writing, it was much more common to do case books and teaching materials rather than scholarly research articles. That was the old school, especially in state law schools. When Bill and I were hired, that was part of a gradual movement toward more academic writing, writing more theoretical articles in law reviews."

This shift in emphasis made Skip even more the odd man out, and not only with the conservative members of the faculty. "There's a propensity to over simplify on the conservative/liberal," mused Nagel, who is looked on as a conservative in the stereotypical sense. Some of those critical of Skip were "pretty standard academic leftist," according to Nagel. "They disapproved of some of Skip's litigating, partly on the grounds of conflict of interest of a state employee, as Skip was, bringing lawsuits against the state and by that, jeopardizing the school's interest for his own selfish purposes, and partly on the grounds that Skip was too much a pain in the ass."

Nagel paused to think back to those times. "I don't think it had to do with Skip's politics. Maybe to some extent, but more with his style—not coming to work dressed up. It offended the old school style. A lot of the faculty was very old school and they believed in a more structured kind of workday than what Skip had. He was a free spirit and these other guys came to work in a suit. They worked hard all day and didn't sue the state.

"Skip was obviously a very ideological person, but he never made it personal. I always appreciated that about him. In that sense, he was 'old school'. It's funny to describe Skip that way. But for a lot of those old school professors, like Dean Courtland Peterson, the politics wasn't personal. It didn't shape the whole world. They could be interested in your academic writing just for the sake of your academic writing. Skip was old school that way. Today, ideology tends to dominate everything. You can't keep it in its box, and this is true in the academic world."

On his office door, Skip had tacked a cartoon showing a Grinch suing to have Christmas tree lights taken down. "It seemed to me he was making fun of himself, that's how far he'd go through litigation," Nagel said. "He thought that's the way people thought of him. I thought that was a nice side of him, that he could see how others might resent his litigations."

Bill Pizzi, who was hired as part of the cultural shift within the CU Law School, echoes Nagel's sentiments about Skip. "What I appreciated and loved about Skip was this bond and affection and respect. I got a kick out of what he was doing. I thought some of his lawsuits were nutty, like suing the Boulder jail so they would have organic peanut butter, those kinds of things. I thought it was a waste of money but that was the legal system. To me, Skip was using the constitution, the separation of church and state, the right of free speech. He was a committed ACLU sort of person."

Skip's activism in the form of lawsuits irritated members of the state legislature to the point where a footnote was inserted into a budget bill appropriating funds to the University of Colorado that said, in effect, state funds or resources, which included personnel time, office space or office supplies, could not be used in the service of bringing a suit against the state. The obscure footnote is colloquially known as the "Skip Chase Amendment."

"That was clearly directed at Skip for his ACLU work more than with his CRLS legal aid because he was suing the state," Jon Asher confirmed. "People in the legislature got tired of it. They said you cannot both take a law school salary and go around suing the state. There are arguments that such a view violates freedom of speech, but Congress has imposed all sorts of limitations on what legal aid lawyers can do, and, with one exception, said we could not challenge welfare reform. Government has said that the power of the purse allows it to set limits on what lawyers can do and that has been upheld all the way to U.S. Supreme Court. It may be immoral and totally inappropriate, but it's not unconstitutional or illegal."

The concept of equal justice under law is firmly embedded in our nation's notion of democracy, yet is a widely violated legal principle, especially in matters of race, gender and poverty. Deborah Rhodes, Stanford law professor and director of the Stanford Center on Ethics, commented on the current state of affairs in an *Ethics at Noon* presentation published by Santa Clara University:

> *"An estimated four-fifths of the legal needs of the poor, and the needs of two to three-fifths of middle-income individuals, remain unmet. Over the past two decades, national spending on legal aid has been cut by a third, and increasingly restrictions have been placed on cases and clients that government-funded programs can accept. Entire categories of the 'unworthy poor' have been denied assistance, and court has largely acquiesced in these limitations, as well as in ludicrous limitations on fees for court appointed lawyers in criminal cases."*

When Ronald Reagan became president in 1981, he attempted to eliminate legal services across the country. As governor of California in the 1960s, Reagan advocated for the end of federal subsides for free legal services to the poor in civil cases. He tried to block a federal grant to the California Rural Legal Assistance in 1970, the organization that inspired Bill Prakken to join with Skip in forming CRLS. *Time* magazine reported that, "Of all the social programs growing out of the Great Society, there is none that Ronald Reagan dislikes more than the Legal Services Corporation."

Legal Services Corporation (LSC), the organizational descendant of the Office of Economic Opportunity that funded CRLS, is a private, non-profit corporation established by Congress in 1974. Rather than asking Congress to disband LSC, Reagan simply cut its funding from the federal budget. Two hundred lawyers, led by American Bar Association president W. Reece Smith, Jr., descended on Washington to fight the threat. The U.S. House Judiciary Committee blocked Reagan's move, but did cut LSC financing to $260 million for both of the next two years. Additional restrictions were placed on the type of cases LSC lawyers could undertake. The following year, 1982, new rules prohibited LSC from trying most class action suits and from lobbying. Reagan administration officials accused LSC of having "concealed and understated" its lobbying activity and support for politically motivated legislation.

"We are more restricted," attested Jon Asher, head of Colorado Legal Service, "because we continue to received federal funds and Congress finally caught on that not only can they limit what we do with their money, they can say, 'If you take our money, you have to agree not to use anybody else's money in ways we don't want.' So we cannot do class action anymore. We cannot represent immigrants, with some exceptions. We cannot do prison cases. There's lot of things we can't do.

"I like to think that we, legal services, infuse much of the work we do but the enemies of the good have gotten much more sophisticated in how to fight us."

Chapter 11

Skip, Dean of Vermont Law School

Anthony N. Doria, the founder of Vermont Law School, was a crook with a prison record to prove it. An Italian immigrant, Doria, a small dapper man with a fondness for tailored Italian suits and beautiful young women adorning his arm at VLS events, could sweet talk water from a rock. Armed with the three Cs necessary for a successful con man—charm, confidence and chutzpah—Doria bamboozled a vulnerable widow out of $115,250 and took in some of the most respected attorneys in Vermont.

Doria came to Vermont because of problems in Pennsylvania—he had been convicted of embezzlement concerning a travel agency he operated. As a way to reestablish himself, he decided to start a private "academy" and drove around Vermont looking for a suitable site. In South Royalton he found a 1892 Victorian school house for sale, as the town needed to build a new elementary school. He purchased the building and advertised nationally and internationally his Royalton Academy, specializing in international students.

The small village of South Royalton, affectionately called So Ro by the inhabitants, was an unlikely place to establish a "school of international relations" as Doria grandly called his creation. The burg was so small it didn't have a stoplight, the nearest one being twenty-seven miles away. The village still doesn't have a stoplight.

Doria accepted entrance fees but in many cases never admitted the students, or returned the fees. As an immigrant, he understood that students from overseas could feel hampered in pursuing their case against him; they might feel insecure in a foreign system, didn't know the proper channels to file claims and perhaps didn't have the language skills to make a case. Nevertheless, he felt the need for better cover. In 1973, he converted the Royalton Academy into the Vermont Law School, the only school in the state to give out law degrees. To give the school legitimacy, he recruited Thomas M. Debevoise, elected as Vermont's Attorney General in 1960, to form a Board of Trustees.

Upon examining the school's books and operations, Debevoise and the Board of Trustees promptly removed Doria and appointed Debevoise as the dean and school's president. However, Doria did not fade away with his tail between his legs. He continued to live to South Royalton, which presented a social conundrum—as the founder and first dean of VLS, should he be invited to school functions, be given a place of honor on the stage?

In 1978, Doria presented the school another contretemps. Dick Brooks, a highly respected environmental attorney, came to VLS and established a summer school as part of the Environmental Law Center. In response, Doria announced the founding of a summer school focused on environmental law, although he had no faculty. However, he did have a building.

"I was suddenly deluged with all these calls," Brooks said. "People were totally mixed up between our school and his school. His school was totally phony. There was no school at all."

Doria put himself up as a Republican candidate for the U.S. Senate in 1982 but dropped out of the race before the primary. Four years later, he ran for the U.S. Senate Republican nomination, losing to former Gov. Richard Snelling, who then lost to incumbent Democratic Sen. Patrick Leahy.

In 2001, the FBI and IRS opened investigations into Doria's financial shenanigans. Two years later, he was indicted by a federal grand jury for defrauding Barbara Umbrecht, a widow in Newport, New Hampshire, of $115,250 over a two-year period through a phony investment scheme. The indictment included one count of mail fraud and four counts of transporting stolen property.

Umbrecht met Doria when she sold him a refrigerator. At the time, Umbrecht, a homemaker, was "very vulnerable," according to her attorney, following her husband's death in 1998. "She didn't even know what she had for assets," said the attorney Lisa Wellman-Ally, and began to sell off personal possessions to support herself. Sensing an opportunity, Doria turned on the charm to gain her confidence. Umbrecht granted him power of attorney. He talked her into signing checks over to him, giving him items of value and selling stocks: he promised to invest the money in the North American Finance and Investment Co. However, he failed to mention that in 1996 the company had been terminated as a corporation allowed to conduct business by the Vermont Secretary of State's Office and would not be reinstated until April 2000.

According to the federal indictment, Doria cashed large checks from Umbretch between November 1998 and January 2000 for his own use or deposited them into a personal account. An indictment is a way of bringing formal charges and is not proof of guilt. To avoid a trial, Doria promised to repay Umbrecht. When he failed to make good, Umbrecht's attorneys filed federal charges against Doria, including manipulating Umbrecht into applying for credit cards that he used for his own purposes.

In March 2004, the federal grand jury added six counts of money laundering to the indictment. If convicted, Doria faced a maximum of 145 years in jail and a fine of $4.2 million. He pleaded guilty to a lesser charge of tax evasion of $21,000 in July 2005 and faced a maximum five-year prison sentence and a $250,000 fine. The 78-year-old Doria was given one month in jail, five months home confinement, three-years probation on the federal tax evasion charges and ordered to make restitutions to Umbrecht.

Despite the notorious background of its founder, Vermont Law School is a highly respected independent law school accredited by the American Bar Association and renowned for its environmental law program and emphasis on public service law. In 2009, *U.S. News and World Report* rated the school as number one in environmental law. The law school has never been ranked lower than number two since the ratings began in 1991.

VLS's president and Dean Tom Debevoise, who had worked night and day to build up the school's finances and establish its good reputation, wanted to retire in 1982. The school sought for the new dean an academic, someone young with fresh ideas and with enthusiasm to move the school forward. A replacement search was instigated and a suitable candidate found when the school received Skip's late application.

"Is this guy really serious?" Professor Dick Brooks, co-chair of the hiring committee, remembered hearing a committee member exclaim. "But, on the other hand, he obviously had accomplished a lot. Jonathon was an interesting candidate, so we gave his candidacy very serious consideration and ultimately selected him. He was hired in reaction to having had a dean for a number of years who basically was a button up kind of guy, very successful but not engaging. Tom was a real Old New Englander. A combination of Jonathon's personality, his record as a litigator and the fact he was an academic coming out of the University of Colorado Law School—all these things operated to having him hired."

The law school faculty at CU was surprised when Skip got the deanship. "That was a real toss for a guy who came to work in jeans and was interested in suing the state prison system," said Bob Nagel. "I'm not saying he wasn't connected to the life of the law school, he was, but not in the way you'd think of as a dean. I was surprised he wanted to do it and surprised there was a law faculty that wanted to hire him. You could regard him as a very pleasant guy and useful to the school, and I still do not think of him as someone who is going to become a dean."

On his first day as the third dean of Vermont Law School, Skip appeared on campus wearing a Mickey Mouse t-shirt. "Most of the faculty, perhaps all the faculty, were absolutely delighted," Brooks said with a laugh. "But all the staff were totally aghast. They felt this was not suitable to the dignity of the dean."

"Skip's experience was the kind of thing the faculty was looking for," stated Karin Sheldon, former Director of the Environmental Law Center, Associate Dean for Environmental Law program and a professor at VLS from1994 to 2007. "When you see the early pictures of the faculty of VLS, they all looked like they had gone back to the land, big bushy beards and long sideburns and not many suits. They looked like hippies gone back to Vermont and founded a law school."

When Skip assumed the deanship, he tried to revert back to Jonathon, regarding "Skip" as not deanly enough. Besides, his wife Nancy really never liked the nickname. Nevertheless, he was generally known as Skip around campus.

As dean, he set about creating a sense of community that didn't exist at the school. Most of the faculty, including Skip and Nancy,

Jonathon Chase as Dean of Vermont Law School. Photo taken sometime in the 1980s. Photo courtesy the Vermont Law School Communications Department

didn't live in South Royalton, suitable housing being limited. VLS was a fractured school with no campus center, dorms, gym or health center. Students gathered at the Crossroads Bar & Grill, literally across the railroad tracks from the school, with its pool tables, video games, a small dance floor and two outdoor horseshoe pitches. One patron described the place as "Beer taps probably haven't been cleaned in a couple decades. The bathrooms stink. The food is mediocre. The spirit of the place and the people who go there make the whole thing worthwhile."

Speaking from his law office in Montpelier, Vermont, Scott Cameron, a member of the VLS Board of Trustees when Skip was hired, said, "Jonathon was trying to figure out how to be a dean. He was trying to figure out how this young law school could survive. It was very difficult times. We were just trying to develop our niche in environmental law, but we did not have it yet, and the economy was bad. He was taking notes, looking around at a lot of different ways to brand the school, how to make it work."

Skip set himself two immediate goals: creating community at VLS and establishing an identity for the law school. "One of the things that he latched on to sell the school was a campaign basically preparing lawyers not for Wall Street but for Main Street," Cameron stated. "VLS was not going to be sending lawyers to the top Wall Street or New York firms and the big bucks. Our lawyers were going to Main Street, to small towns and communities all over the country to practice law and provide services for regular people, small businesses."

His mission statement to students was "we're going to give you a solid grounding and prepare you to practice law from day one rather than go carry someone's bag for $100,000 a year for five years for some big firm that overcharges their corporate clients," according to Cameron. "He was trying to be very honest. During his tenure, he expanded our experiential programs, our legal clinics and put resources there and put resources into experiential courses like appellate advocacy and advanced trial practice, NITA courses. Our students were not just studying case law but doing hands-on work and being prepared to start practicing law as soon as they got out, which was generally in a Main Street type of environment or public sector.

"Tom Debevoise put the school on a solid business foundation. Skip was more a visionary guy. He was very interested in preparing young people to go out and work in public interest. He'd often urged

Jonathon Chase teaching at Vermont Law School, sometime in the 1980s.
Photo courtesy the Vermont Law School Communications Department

students to try and do that in their first year or two of law practice. I remember him saying to do the public service before you get that comfortable job. If you have a passion, something you are really interested in, do it now before you get bogged down with the house, the dog, the kids. Do it while you are free and you can take a chance, go out and do something that you believe in. He had such an influence on students. He put more energy into the students than he put in cultivating the board, even the faculty.

"Our students still remain tremendously interested in public interest and go on to work in, not just environmental organizations, but public sector and public interest jobs all over the country," Cameron said. "We are now referred to as one of the top twenty public interest law schools. That goes back to Jonathon's early influence."

But Skip got off to a somewhat rocky start with the faculty, according to Brooks. He resisted associating the law school with environmental groups, which a number of the teachers advocated.

"This would have shielded the school from any potential conflicts between litigation on one hand and, let's say, fund raising on the other hand," Brooks said. "Both the Conservation Law Foundation of Boston and the Vermont Natural Resources Council, of which I had been a board member, were very interested in working with VLS. Jonathon balked. He didn't want anything that was not a clinic on campus, anything that was not supervised by faculty or carried out by the law school itself. I was disappointed in Jonathon in that regard. He wanted the whole pie or none of it. As a consequence, the environmental law clinic didn't start to get established for some years later. Now we have a very full environmental clinic, but, as I say, it is curious, given his commitment, that it didn't flower during his particular position while he was here."

A couple years into his tenure, Skip caused another controversy on campus—he banned the U.S. military Judge Advocate General from interviewing students on campus. Some students protested Skip was depriving them of a job opportunity. His response: gays and lesbians were excluded from serving in the military and discrimination was against the school's policy. Therefore, he was not allowing the recruiters on campus. The upset students wanted to address the Board of Trustees and have Skip's decision overturned.

"Jonathon" cartoon featured in the Vermont Law School Forum.
Photo courtesy the Vermont Law School Communications Department

Prior to banning the military recruiters from campus, he had not advised the board about his policy; the board was a very patriotic group, many of the members having served in World War II and the Korean War. The agitated students attended a Board of Trustees meeting, at which Skip was present.

"The students' complaint hit the board by surprise," Cameron, on the board of trustees at the time, recalled. "You can imagine the consternation, the upset students, board members not understanding why this had happened, why we were not allowing the military to recruit, because we supported our country and we supported our students getting jobs. Jonathon was, by then, on the defense trying to explain and defend his decision."

Skip stoutly and passionately spoke out for the principle of non-discrimination and equality, the bedrock of his philosophy. The discussion caused turmoil around the board table until, according to Cameron, Tom Debevoise, the trustee emeritus, a crusty old guy with a smoker's voice, said, "Jonathon, you say you made this decision because of our non-discrimination policy. Well, Jonathon, I am looking at the non-discrimination policy and our policy does not address sexual preferences."

A silence fell over the room. "Jonathon is swallowing his Adam's apple at that point," said Cameron, who sat at the board table. "Then Tom Debevoise says, 'I think someone should make a motion to add sexual orientation to our non-discrimination policy.' If you knew Tom and his conservative background, you wouldn't have expected that. But he thought it was the right thing to do and the right thing was to support Jonathon. A motion was made and the Board unanimously voted to add sexual orientation to our non-discrimination policy and to support Jonathon's decision."

VLS was one of two law schools in the country to refuse cooperation with the 1966 Solomon Amendment, a statute passed by Congress requiring college and universities to allow military recruitment on campus or risk losing federal funding. As a result, the school gave up over a million dollars in federal funding.

The school was (and is) also a member of FAIR, Forum for Academic and Institutional Rights, a consortium of thirty-eight law schools and law faculties that challenged the Solomon Amendment in Rumsfeld v. FAIR, claiming that the military's "Don't Ask, Don't Tell" policy regarding gays in the military was discriminatory. This policy was reversed by the Obama administration in 2010.

The legacy of Skip's stance against discrimination was strongly felt years after. "Every year we (the faculty) would have a conversation about it," said Karin Sheldon the former director of the VLS Environmental Law Center. (She now teaches environmental law at the University of Colorado Law School and is the Executive Director of the Western Resources Advocates, a non-profit environmental organization.) "There was always the idea that our anti-discrimination policy was costing the school money, that we were being deprived of grants and so on. I was proud of the deans and faculty during my tenure for stating, 'We don't care. We think this is an important policy statement.' The students could talk to the military if they wanted, and we had students who did, but we were not going to have military on campus recruiting."

Jonathon Chase with Vermont Law School rugby team. Photo taken in 1984.
Courtesy the Vermont Law School Communications Department

VLS graduate Rosemarie Russo (Class of 1986) remembers her time on campus during Skip's tenure as a "good balance of intellectual rigor, friendship, general interest in the law and doing good work in the environmental field. VLS did promote public service advocacy and 'ecosystem' advocacy, which was fairly progressive in 1985. Most of my peers were focused more on doing good rather than making money. I think Skip's leadership helped set VLS apart from some other cutthroat competitive law schools in the country, although there was a strong competition element in all the courses.

"Skip was a wonderful combination of intellectual and humanitarian. As a dean, he played rugby, looked youthful and vigorous, was energetic, approachable, accessible and down to earth. He wasn't the 'behind-the-desk' authoritative figure that is disconnected from faculty and students. I worked as a dean for about a decade and followed in his footsteps in being approachable and setting an example of a strong work ethic.

"What impressed me about Skip was he'd be out running in below zero temperatures. He exemplified that people need to keep a balance between the physical and the intellectual. He'd get muddy, down and dirty in a rugby game. He wasn't a big guy but he was tough and passionate about rugby."

Russo now teaches Sustainability and Environmental Law at the CU Law School, Boulder, and acts as the Sustainability Coordinator for Ft. Collins, Colorado.

But Skip's style caused a kerfuffle—again—when Elliot L. Richardson was given an honorary degree by VLS.

As the U.S. Attorney General under President Richard Nixon, Richardson refused Nixon's instructions to fire Special Prosecutor Archibald Cox, who was investigating Nixon in the Watergate scandal. Richardson resigned in protest and was hailed as a moral hero. At the presentation dinner, Skip seated Richardson in what he regarded as the place of honor, right next to the bandstand, where Skip, wearing a t-shirt, played the bongos. Richardson, very much a New England Brahmin and former Harvard law professor, was horrified, according to Brooks.

"The look on his face, like, 'What did I get myself into'," Brooks recalled with a smile. "After five minutes, he walked out and Jonathon could care less. He just kept on playing those bongos. It was great, the clash of cultures. Those who knew Jonathon were just totally delighted because he was such an effervescent guy. He was just phenomenal."

Overall, Skip got mixed reviews as dean. He raised money for the new Cornell Library, the general practice program and for other projects. He enthusiastically represented the school and gave it spirit. On the flip side: "Jonathon was a horrible manager," according to Brooks. "He was not good. In fact, he was not renewed as dean after the first four or five years. I feel bad about this in a way. He came to me and begged me to back his candidacy for a second term. I said, 'Jonathon, you're a lovely guy and I hope you will be my colleague for life.' But, you know he could never sit back and listen to contending forces, which you have to do as a dean. You have to be judicious and handle people. Jonathon could never assume that distance. He never mastered that aspect of deaning at all. He would always leap in, combative no matter what, and would pick a side and just push. He was guaranteed to alienate a large number of the faculty, and did."

In the winter of 1987, Skip thought he had caught a cold, not an unreasonable assumption in Vermont. As the feeling of congestion in his chest persisted, a nagging that never went away, he blamed it on allergies. Even the increasing tiredness was attributed to a lingering minor ailment. Finally, he consulted a doctor. A lemon-size tumor was found in his chest. He had successfully battled a bout of testicular cancer while living in Colorado, but now the scourge reappeared. This cancer was inoperable.

"I went to see him at his house after he was diagnosed with lung cancer," Scott Cameron said. "We were good friends, played lacrosse together, at which he was a lot better than me. Skip was a tremendous athlete. They called him Captain Mogul in skiing. In rugby he was competitive in a fun healthy way, not negative. He looked good the day I visited. He couldn't get rid of this cough, he said, and had a

Jonathon Chase at a function in Vermont in the 1980s. Photo courtesy the Vermont Law School Communications Department

tumor in his lung. He had this look on his face like, 'How could this happen?' He wasn't feeling sorry for himself but bemused. He couldn't believe he had lung cancer. The cancer was such an aberration. He never smoked, was healthy."

Still, the cancer didn't dampen his enthusiasm for life. Despite the chemotherapy, he remained as active as the debilitating treatment allowed. He wrestled with Adam; on a bike trip he visited his old CRLS colleague Judge John Kuenhold in Alamosa, Colorado; he stopped in

Boulder to see his friend Bill Cohen. "He had a shaved head, which made him look like a handsome Yul Brenner," Cohen recalled. "When we hugged, he felt solid and robust. He was in good spirits."

Brooks visited Skip at a time when his life was clearly coming to an end. "He was quite convivial, despite the fact he was having significant breathing problems," recalled Brooks. "He was not bedridden or anything like that. He was a very strong man, barrel-chested, a tough guy."

Linda, Skip's sister, came to visit her dying brother and wrote this poignant poem:

In Rural Vermont

I have slipped past a spinning wheel,
a butter churn and a large dog, to sit here
in the bentwood rocking chair beside your bed.
We must be the remains of Early Americans
who look out the windows at bare maple trees
and the sides of barns through slatted blinds.
Winter, snow, the sound of a car from time to time,
four wheel drive, snow tyres whistling down the road.
The houses are close to the road in rural Vermont.
How else would we ever get out in winter.

The New York Times is spread across your chest,
Vermont Courier at your side, briefcase, papers.
Beside you, cards, letters, flowers, the telephone.
A glass of water is full, the straw has been renewed.
I wouldn't dream of touching a thing as you sleep.

In the late afternoon, I field a phone call from a friend,
though I am to wake you if they call from the Court House.
State's rights, Federal law, something about dentists.

The runners of my chair on the braided rug,
rocking, pad the sound of your bound breath.
I'm glad this chair was left so close to the bed.
I wouldn't want to move the furniture to be close to you.
Our mother's quilt is bunched a little at your feet,
But for the life of me, I leave it.

On December 5, 1987, a cold grey Friday, Skip died, at the age of 48, of lung cancer in his home in Norwich, Vermont. "I was told a story," Brooks recalled, "that he said good night to his friends and went up stairs. In the middle of the night, he couldn't breathe any longer or call out. Then he died."

His funeral was held at Dartmouth College, which had the only auditorium in the area large enough to accommodate the over 1,000 people who attended. Skip's old friend, former Sen. Tim Wirth, now at the United Nation's Foundation, was one of those who eulogized Skip at the service. At the memorial, Scott Cameron spoke to his friend by reading a verse from Robert Graves' free verse translation of the *Rubaiyat of Omar Khayyaam*:

Jonathon, your mortal carcass is a tent
Your soul, a Sultan
Your camp, you move.

The groom named Fate calls out the march
And strikes the tent when
Sultan-like, you move.

Jonathon when you are free
to shed your mortal carcass
and soar freely across God's great empyrean
You will blush to think you lay so long in body's jail.

After her husband's death, Nancy continued to live in Norwich. She considered becoming a teacher in religion and attended a teacher-training institute, but decided teaching wasn't for her. She sold the large house and now lives in a small, very eloquent house on top of a steep hill. She has many women friends in the area but, according to Brooks, "has pretty much turned away from the law school and is not very much involved anymore."

In Skip's memory, the VLS Founder's Library was renamed the Jonathon B. Chase Community Center, which serves as the student center. A Jonathon Chase Memorial Scholarship was established to benefit students holding positions in the ACLU, various public defenders' offices and other advocacy groups. The scholarship speaks to the very heart of VLS's mission of advocacy in civil rights, public interest and social justice. The sense at VLS is that the scholarship is vital to the future of both the school and the country to cultivate the next generation of lawyer-advocates.

Every year the Annual Chase Race, a 5K fun run, is held at VLS with proceeds funding a scholarship for students seeking to pursue careers in public interest law. Skip's son Adam has participated in the race.

The Dean Jonathon B. Chase Paper is awarded each year by the *Vermont Law Review* to a third year student whose submitted entry best represents the standards established by Dean Chase and continued by the *Vermont Law Review*.

The Jonathon B. Chase Community Center on the Vermont Law School campus in South Royalton, Vermont. The former Vermont Law School Founder's Library was renamed in his honor following his death on December 5, 1987 at age 48. Photo courtesy the Vermont Law School Communications Department

The University of Colorado Law School established the Jonathon B. Chase Human Rights Fellowship in 1988, available to CU Law School students to work with underprivileged people. Fifty students have been given the scholarship award since its inception. Robert Retherford, who received the fellowship in 2002, used the money to intern at the Southern Ute Tribal Court for a summer.

"That deepened my interest in and knowledge of Indian law," Retherford said. "I did research and wrote briefs for the three tribal judges on a wide variety of legal issues, worked on tribal codes, and organized their library. The Chase Fellowship gave me the freedom to put my legal training to work without having to worry about how I was going to eat or pay my rent that summer. I appreciate having had the Fellowship's support so I could do pro bono work for a worthy cause. It also definitely helped shape where I have gone in my legal profession."

Retherford, based in Aztec, N.M., is an active member of the Navajo Nation Bar and the New Mexico Bar associations and has done work with the Jicarilla Apache tribe.

At a memorial service for Skip at the University of Colorado, Jean Dubofsky eulogized her friend, colleague and mentor.

"Skip practiced what he believed in his life. His signature law suits, like the early farm worker cases he brought in the federal district court in Denver, grew out of his own experience doing work in the fields, out of actually meeting the people. They were not abstract notions. His cases were like nothing anyone had seen in a federal court before. He'd take on anyone.

"The early years of CRLS had a romantic quality. The sense that one could make a difference, one could make the world better. The program, as it began, was really a reflection of Skip, a romantic character if ever there was one. The dictionary defines romantic as 'attentive, heroic, and picturesque'. The early romantic quality of the program quickly gave way to militancy that ended Skip's years as director without an opportunity for many people to say, 'Thank you. You did a super job.' He left a very solid base for people who represent farm workers and low-income clients in rural Colorado. He handled adversity, including his own death, with incredible grace."

Bill Cohen, colleague, friend and original CRLS board member, gave the best epitaph for Skip: *tikkun olam*, a major concept in Judaism meaning "repairing the world."

"*Tikkun olam* is working in this life for good, to make the world better," Cohen explained. "That was the essence of Skip Chase."

Skip Chase

Here's to a dreamer
Who saw the future
      And all the worlds that
         Could be found

      And opened

    Sometimes late at night
        He wanted to leave early
          And jump right into tomorrow.

And he wanted tomorrow
      To become better
Than the predicted forecast
      He practiced magic
    Pulling more than rabbits
      Out of his bag of tricks
Believing in something called justice
      He built a team
Of like dreamers
    They came and talked of hope
    And winning
      Long before the games would begin.
    These assembled super stars
    would defend
The poorest of the poor
    Against some who had
    More money than morals.

The powerless

                        Facing off against the powerful.
        Davids and Dianas
against so many Goliaths.

        Skip's team's compensation
          In the end
        Was knowing that they
      Had fought the noblest of fights
        For the right reasons
             And against impossible odds...

        It wasn't easy
           It wasn't safe
It wasn't always clean
           But in the end
They opened doors
   and windows

        Exposing
          A better road
          Into the future
          And taught others
       Why they must dream
   and do

        What some
            Would think is impossible.

Skip led his fellow explorers
On this historic journey
Guided by some inner compass
That drove some crazy
And inspired almost everyone
who would drink of his vision

Of hope and change.

—Len Rose-Avila

Jonathon Chase playing bongos in a band in Vermont.
Photo taken in the 1980s, courtesy the Vermont Law
School Communications Department

Appendix A

Summary of Proposals

In 1967, Skip testified before Secretary of Agriculture Orville Freeman on the problems of migrant farm workers in sugar beets. He recommended that the minimum hourly wage for sugar beet workers be raised to $2.00 per hour in 1968.

At the conclusion of the *Colorado Law Review* article, he listed a summary of his proposals to address the persistent and, in his opinion, unfair labor practices suffered by migrant workers.

1. The Secretary of Agriculture should require that workers in sugar beets be given their choice of the hourly or piece rate minimum, whichever is greater; but in no case should the producer be permitted to pay less than the hourly minimum.

2. The Colorado Industrial Commission should set minimum wages for women and children employed in agricultural labor.

3. The Secretary of Agriculture should require producers of sugar beets to pay workers directly.

4. The Wage and Hour Division of the United States Department of Labor should take a far more active role in enforcing the Fair Labor Standards acts, including the education of growers and workers as to the scope of the act and independent investigations to determine the existence of violations.

5. The Bureau of Employment Security of the United States Department of Labor should enforce the Farm Labor Contractor

Appendix A: Summary of Proposals

Registration Act of 1963, particularly that portion of the Act relating to misrepresentation by the contractor to his workers of the terms of employment, by undertaking their own investigations to discover violations.

6. The Colorado Department of Employment, Farm Placement Office, should cease recruiting through contractors and recruit only heads of families or individual workers. Those companies which undertake their own recruitment should do the same.

7. Local State Employment Offices ought to begin to serve some useful function in the areas of farm labor by becoming clearing houses where farmers in need of workers and workers in need of jobs can go to find one another.

8. The Colorado legislature should enact into law the regulations applicable to labor camps adopted by the Colorado Department of Health so that criminal sanctions would be available to enforce compliance with minimal standards of health and decency.

9. The Colorado Department of Employment, Farm Placement Office, should do as it says it does and stop recruiting for growers who do not meet the standards set by the Colorado Department of Health for the housing of workers.

10. The Secretary of Agriculture should require that, as a condition to receiving sugar payments, producers who undertake to provide housing for their workers must provide housing which is adequate.

11. Congress should amend the National Labor Relations Act so as to include agricultural labor.

12. The Colorado legislature should extend to agricultural labor the protections afforded other workers by removing the exemption of agriculture labor from the Labor Peace Act, Workmen's Compensations and Employment Security.

13. The Colorado legislature should remove the requirement of residency as a condition to eligibility for welfare programs.

14. The Colorado bar should support and aid in the development and implementation of a vital, creative statewide rural legal assistance program.

Appendix B

Cases Litigated by Jonathon B. Chase

Benoni v. Boston & Maine Corp., 828 F.2d 52 (1st Cir. 1987)

Challenged employee's discharge for alleged role in an unauthorized and illegal work stoppage. Court upheld the discharge finding the claim of discriminatory discharge to be timed barred and that Benoni had failed to allege a cause of action under Private Law 98-9.

Razatos v. Colorado Supreme Court, 746 F.2d 1429 (10th Cir. 1984)

Challenged the dismissal, for lack of subject matter jurisdiction, of an action seeking declaratory judgment that the Colorado procedure for disciplining lawyers was in violation of due process. Court held that jurisdiction was proper for the constitutional challenge, but that the current disciplinary procedures contained safeguards sufficient to protect due process rights.

Razatos v. Colorado Supreme Court, 549 F.Supp. 789 (D. Colo. 1982)

Plaintiff sought declaratory judgment that the Colorado Rule of Civil Procedure 252 violated the due process clause. Court held that it did not have original jurisdiction over the claim, that the plaintiff failed to raise a federal question, and that the rule did not violate due process.

Citizens Concerned for Separation of Church & State v. City & County of Denver, 526 F.Supp 1310 (D. Colo. 1981)

Citizens' association sought to prevent the display of a nativity scene as part of a Christmas lightning display arguing that it was in violation of the Establishment Clause of the First Amendment. Court found for the defendant holding that the lightning display did not have the direct and immediate effect of advancing or inhibiting religion.

Gurule v. Wilson, 525 F.Supp. 996 (D. Colo 1981)

Both parties appealed the award of attorney fees. Court held that it was proper to consider Mr. Chase's use of law school facilities as an overhead expense paid by the state when determining a reasonable fee award. Court awarded $6,007.50 in fees for Mr. Chase's legal services.

Citizens Concerned for Separation of Church & State v. City & County of Denver, 508 F.Supp. 823 (D. Colo. 1981)

Court denied motion for a preliminary injunction. See similar cite above for facts.

Gurule v. Wilson, 649 F.2d 754 (10th Cir. 1981)

Both parties appealed the award of attorney fees. Court held that it may proportionally reduce a requested attorney's fee for time spent on substantial separate issues which are raised but which ultimately fail.

Chiappe v. State Personnel Bd., 662 P.2d 527 (Colo. 1981)

Petitioners sought review of a State Personnel Board ruling on the termination of food service workers for failing to comply with the "no-beard" rule. Court affirmed the termination on several grounds stating that the liberty interest in selecting one's appearance is much less significant than other constitutional liberties.

Appendix B: Cases Litigated by Jonathon B. Chase

Gurule v. Wilson, 635 F.2d 782 (10th Cir. 1980)

Procedural challenges related to attorney fees and class certification.

Wesson v. Johnson, 622 P.2d 104 (Colo. App. 1980)

Challenged the denial of an application for an award of attorney fees made under the Civil Rights Attorney's Fees Award Act. Court affirmed holding that trial court lack jurisdiction to consider the application.

Citizens Concerned for Separation of Church & State v. City & County of Denver, 628 F.2d 1289 (10th Cir. 1980)

Defendants appealed a judgment enjoining the display of a nativity scene at a city and county building. The court dismissed the appeal and vacated the injunction finding that the plaintiffs lacked standing to seek an injunction.

Citizens Concerned for Separation of Church & State v. City and County of Denver, 481 F.Supp. 522 (D. Colo. 1979)

District court found that the display of a nativity scene on public property was in violation of the protection of minority views provide by the Establishment Clause of the First Amendment. Court enjoined the nativity scene from being displayed.

Wesson v. Bowling, 604 P.2d 23 (Colo. 1979)

Writ of mandamus sought to compel the district court to enter a written order requiring county sheriff to implement contact visitation program with pretrial detainees. Court held that minute order approval of the regulations was effective as a written order and was therefore binding regardless of failure of the court to restate the regulations in a written order.

Marioneaux v. Colorado State Penitentiary, 465 F.Supp. 1245 (D. Colo. 1979)

Maximum security inmates brought a class action challenging the placement of inmates in punitive and administrative segregation alleging violations of due process. Court granted a temporary restraining order holding that housing reorganization was insufficient justification for failing to comply with prison procedures regarding inmates transfers.

Wesson v. Johnson, 579 P.2d 1165 (Colo. 1978)

Pretrial detainees in county jail brought a civil rights action claiming they had been denied a constitutional right to a program of contact visitation. Court found that areas of the jail could be used for contact visitation without impairing security and remanded the case in order of the trial court to require the sheriff to implement a contact visitation program.

Doe v. Pringle, 550 F.2d 596 (10th Cir. 1976)

Challenge to the denial of admission to the Colorado bar after receiving favorable recommendation from the bar committee. The court affirmed the denial holding that it did not have subject matter jurisdiction to hear the claim.

Skafte v. Rorex, 553 P.2d 830 (Colo. 1976)

Constitutional challenge to Colorado statutes that deny aliens the right to vote in school elections. Court upheld the statutes finding that the citizenship requirement does not violate equal protection or due process.

Appendix B: Cases Litigated by Jonathon B. Chase

Goldsmith v. Pringle, 399 F.Supp 620 (D. Colo. 1975)

Attorney challenged Colorado bar reciprocity rule prohibiting admission by motion where the reciprocal state also prohibits admission by motion. The court upheld the rule, holding that it had a rational basis, was reasonably calculated to further legitimate state objectives, and was not in violation of equal protection rights.

Sandoval v. Ryan, 535 P.2d 244 (Colo. App. 1975)

High school student challenged the constitutionality of high school transfer procedures where they did not provide for a hearing. After withdrawing his claim for injunctive relief, the court found that the lack of a remedy made the question moot and that a class action could not be brought in the student's name.

Montgomery v. Douglas, 388 F.Supp. 1139 (D. Colo. 1974)

Student challenged the Colorado statute which prevents students at state universities from receiving in-state tuition until they have lived in the state for one year. Court upheld the statute finding that it had a rational basis and was reasonably related to a legitimate state interest.

Angel v. Butz, 487 F.2d 260 (10th Cir. 1973)

Sugar beet workers challenged the Secretary of Agriculture's declaration of regulations regarding the workers' wages. The court upheld the regulations finding that the Secretary could reject the demands of the representatives of the workers and that he was without jurisdiction to regulate working conditions other than wage rates.

United Farm Workers Union, AFL-CIO v. Mel Finerman Co., 364 F.Supp. 326 (D. Colo. 1973)

Union sought a preliminary injunction giving union members access to a migrant labor camp. The court issued the injunction against the operator of the camp subject to the protection of the basic constitutional rights of both the operator and the workers.

Spann v. Industrial Commission, 508 P.2d 385 (Colo. 1973)

Plaintiff challenged a decision by the Industrial Commission which denied him unemployment compensation. Court reversed the order and remanded for a new hearing.

Almarez v. Carpenter, 347 F.Supp, 597 (D. Colo. 1972)

Indigents claimed that they were being deprived of due process and equal protection when they were denied a cost-free reporter's transcript on motion for a new trial. Court held that the transcript was unnecessary to permit review and that plaintiffs failed to show that they could not get adequate review under an alternative method of providing an appellate record.

Chavez v. Freshpict Foods Inc., 456 F.2d 890 (10th Cir. 1972)

Domestic farm workers sought the declaration of a private cause of action for the enforcement of immigration laws and damages where their employer had hired Mexican nationals who had illegally entered the United States. The court denied that a private cause existed and refused to award damages.

Freshpict Foods Inc. v. Reynaldo Campos, Orlinda De Vargas, Dicho Y Hecho, 492 P.2d 867 (Colo. App. 1971)

Appeal was sought for the issuance of a temporary restraining order enjoining the defendants from using force, threats, or intimidation to prevent the growing and harvesting of lettuce. Court ruled that the temporary restraining order was not appealable under Colorado Appellate Rules 1(a).

Chavez v. Freshpict Foods Inc., 322 F.Supp. 146 (D. Colo. 1971)

Domestic farm workers brought a claim that they were being deprived of employment by the employment of aliens who had illegally entered the United States. Court held that a private cause action against person employing aliens did not exist and consequently dismissed the case for failure to state a claim.

Almarez v. Carpenter, 477 P.2d 792 (Colo. 1970)

Certified questions on the issue of whether C.R.X. 1963, 33-1-3, which allows a poor person to bring an action without the payment of costs, gives that person a right to a trial transcript without cost. Court found that C.R.S. 1963, 33-1-3 does not give the right to a transcript without cost and that such a denial does not violate provisions of the Colorado Constitution pertaining to equality of justice.

Rodriguez v. Fimbelman, 317 F.Supp. 921 (D. Colo. 1970)

Sugar beet workers sought declaratory judgment that 7 U.S.C. 1131(c) (1) prohibited deductions to be taken out of the plaintiff's wages for the benefit of a third party creditor. The court granted the judgment sought.

Salazar v. Hardin, 314 F.Supp. 1257 (D. Colo. 1970)

A class action on behalf of sugar beet workers challenged the practice of making wage payments to crew leaders and not directly to the workers. The court found such provisions as invalid and inconsistent with the minimum wage provisions of the Sugar Act.

Appendix C

Publications by Jonathon B. Chase

Jonathon B. Chase, *Does Professional Licensing Conditioned upon Mutual Reciprocity Violate the Commerce Clause?*, 10 VT. L. REV. 223 (1985)

Through the analysis of Great Atlantic & Pacific Tea Co. v. Cottrell, Sporhase v. Nebraska ex. rel. Douglas, and Metropolitan Life Ins. Co v. Ward, Mr. Chase argues that states which require mutual reciprocity for bar admission violate the commerce clause of the U.S. Constitution.

Jonathon B. Chase, *The Premature Demise of Irrebuttable Presumptions*, 47 U. COLO. L. REV. 653 (1976)

Discusses the rise of the doctrine of irrebuttable presumptions/ procedural due process and the limiting effect of Weinberger v. Salfi. Mr. Chase argues that the doctrine has merit in cases involving overclassification and imposition on interests in property or liberty.

Jonathon B. Chase, *The Migrant Farmworker in Colorado – The Life and the Law*, 40 U. COL. L. REV. 45 (1976)

Describes the life of migrant farrmworkers in Colorado and his legal difficulties regarding wages, housing, protection under labor laws, and accessibility to legal services. Mr. Chase concluded with a series of proposals aimed at addressing the plight of migrant farmworkers.

Contributors

Norm Aaronson, Jonathan Asher, Magdaleno "Len" Rose-Avila, Richard Brooks, Scott Cameron, Adam Chase, Linda Chase, Frank and Jean Dubofsky, Tep Falcon, David Getches, Dan Israel, John Kuenhold, Jesse Manzanares, Don Miller, Robert Nagel, Bill Pizzi, Bill Prakken, Jennie Sanchez, Karin Sheldon, Shelley Wittevrongel, Jim Zapf

Other Contributors

Trudy Foreman and Jeff Aldred, Maria Susan Aragon, Shawn Collins, Doug Enzor, Sheila Fortune, Pat Furman, Carol Grasse, Janis Judd, Carolyn Oakley, Michael Evans Smith, Mary Ann Wright

Bibliography

Interviews

Jonathan Asher, Dick Brooks, Scott Cameron, Adam Chase, Linda Chase, Bill Cohen, Jean Dubofsky, Tep Falcon, David Getches, Dan Israel, John Kuenhold, Jesse Manzanares, Don Miller, Robert Nagel, Bill Pizzi, Bill Prakken, Robert Retherford, Magdaleno "Len" Rose-Avila, Jennie Sanchez, Karin Sheldon

Print

Colorado Law Review, 45, 1967

Vermont Law School *Forum*, Vol. XVIII, No. 3, Oct. 16, 1992 LawSchool.com

Citizens Concerned for Separation of Church & State v. City & County of Denver, 526 R.Supp. 1310 (D. Colo. 1981)

Gurule v. Wilson, 525, F.Supp. 996 (D. Colo. 1981)

Chiappe v. State Personnel Bd, 622 P.2d 527 (Colo. 1981)

Citizens Concerned for Separation of Church and State v. City & County of Denver, 628, F.2d 1289 (10th Cir. 1980)

Citizens Concerned for Separation of Church and State v. City and County of Denver, 481 F.Supp 522 (D. Colo. 1979)

Angel v. Butz, 487 F.2d 260 (10th Cir. 1973)

Salazar v. Hardin, 314 F.Supp. 1257 (D. Colo. 1970)

Euresti v. Stenner, 458 F.2d 1115 (10th Cir. 1972)

Maryknoll Magazine, 1978

Ethics at Noon presentation by Deborah Rhode, Santa Clara University

New York Times, "Howard Higman, Academic Impresario, Dies at 80," by Robert McG Thomas, Jr., Dec. 1, 1995

Deep Play by Diane Ackerman, Random House, New York, 1999

About the Authors

Stephen Foehr has seven non-fiction and fiction published books, including the biography of the blues legend Taj Mahal (www.stephenfoehr.com) The non-ficiton works center on music as a vehicle to explore the culture and history of a place and its people, for example Cuba and Jamaica. Mr. Foehr's novel, *Storyville*, is based in 1905 New Orleans. Storyville, adjacent to the French Quarter, was the only legally defined red-district in the country and the seedbed of jazz.

George "Ron" Waldie first met Skip Chase in 1968 while working with the Colorado Migrant Council. Mr. Waldie, a graduate of the University of New Mexico, worked with the Migrant Council until 1971, then worked with a similar project in Oregon and Idaho. Later, he worked for the U.S. Postal Service, retiring after twenty-seven years. He lives in Boulder, Colo.

INDEX

A

Aaronson, Norm 11, 80, 169

Ackerman, Diane 36–37, 172

ACLU 129–130, 149

Adams State College 86

AFL-CIO 164

Alicia Patterson Foundation 94

American Civil Liberties Union 122. *See also* ACLU

Amnesty International USA 71

Andrews Sisters, The 77

Annual Chase Race 149

Asher, Jonathan "Jon" 15–16, 33, 35, 88–89, 91, 115, 130–131, 169, 171

B

Baldwin, James 122

Beatles, The 77

Bennington College 31

Biafra 77

Billings, Glen 15

Bowers, Bob 90

Brooks, Richard "Dick" 133, 135–136, 140, 144, 147, 148–149, 169, 171

C

California Rural Legal Assistance (CRLA) 67, 131

Cameron, Scott 169, 171

Carlos, Juan 111

Chase, Adam 3, 22, 27–30, 32, 35–36, 78, 146, 149, 169, 171

Chase, David Boyd 22–23, 27

Chase, Eli 3, 28, 30

Chase, Lillian 22–23, 29

Chase, Linda 3–4, 7, 22–27, 29, 31, 38, 147, 169, 171

Chase, Rebecca 3, 28

Chase, Tamara 3, 28

Chiappe v. State Personnel Board 125, 160, 171

Chicago 7 77

Chomsky, Noam 122

Civil Rights Act 76, 77

Civil Rights Commission 88

CLS 15–16. *See also* Colorado Legal Services (CLS)

CMC. *See* Colorado Migrant Council (CMC)

Colorado College 71

Colorado Council on Migrant and Seasonal Agricultural Workers 95

Colorado Farm Bureau 106–107

Colorado Legal Services (CLS) 15. *See also* Legal Services Corporation (LSC)

Colorado Migrant Council (CMC) 9, 39–40, 49–50, 56–58, 65, 69–71, 93–95, 112, 173

Colorado Rural Legal Services (CRLS) 9–10, 13, 69, 107

Conference on World Affairs 39

Conservation Law Foundation of Boston 140

Corle, Susan (nee McGee) 120

Cornell Library 145

Cox, Archibald 144

Crèche. *See* Denver City and County Nativity Scene

Crested Butte Massacre 18

CRLA. *See* California Rural Legal Assistance (CRLA)

CRLS 9, 13–18, 30, 32–33, 35, 40, 67–68, 70–71, 73–76, 78, 81–82, 86–91, 93–95, 97–99, 100–103, 106–110, 111–117, 118, 124–126, 130–131, 146, 151. *See also* Colorado Rural Legal Services (CRLS)

Crossroads Bar & Grill 137

D

Davis, Mike 68

Dean Jonathon B. Chase Paper 149

Debevoise, Thomas M. 133, 135, 138, 141

Deep Play. *See* Ackerman, Diane

Democratic National Committee 71

Democratic National Convention 77

Denver City and County Nativity Scene 122–125, 160, 161

Denver & Rio Grande Railroad 86

Doria, Anthony N. 132–135

Doyle, William E. 102

Dubofsky, Frank 11, 73, 75, 169

Dubofsky, Jean E. 11, 15–16, 33, 35, 73, 75, 100–102, 151, 169, 171

E

Edwards, Al 46–48, 60

Euresti, Rafaela 16, 172

F

FAIR. *See* Forum for Academic and Institutional Rights

Fair Labor Standards Act 63, 156

Falcon, Ricardo 61, 104

Falcon, Tep 61, 103, 104, 169, 171

Farm Labor Contractor Registration Act 156

federal regulation 7 U.S.C. 1131 (c) (1) 101

First Amendment 77, 123, 160, 161

Forum for Academic and Institutional Rights 142

Freeman, Orville 156

Frutchey, Cecil W. 95

Ft. Hood Three 122

G

Georgetown Law School 73

Getches, David 10, 32, 78–79, 120, 125, 169, 171

GI Civil Liberties Defense Committee 122–123

Ginn, Robert 47–48

Good Shepherd Home for Girls 70

Gourevitch, Philip 77

Granados, Freddy 112

Great Atlantic & Pacific Tea Co. 167

Great Western Sugar Company 60

Green, James 56

Greenstein, Mel 99

Gurule v. Wilson 125, 160, 161, 171

H

Hardin, Clifford 100

Head, Linda 70

Head Start 56, 57, 70, 76

Hendrix, Jimi 77

Herlands, Federal District Judge William B. 38

Herrero, Gregorio 94

Higman, Howard 39–40, 112, 172

Hill-Burton Act 14–17

Hines, George 43–44, 50–51

Holguin, Daniel M. 116

Hunter, Bob 39–40

I

Israel, Dan 34, 123, 169, 171

J

Johnson, Pfc. James 122
Johnson, President Lyndon 9, 76
Jon Asher 35
Jonathon B. Chase Community Center 149
Jonathon B. Chase Human Rights Fellowship 150
Jonathon Chase Memorial Scholarship 149
Jones, Tom 39
Joplin, Janis 77
Judge Advocate General 140

K

Kennedy, President John 77
Kerr, Jim 74
Kittle, Dean 107
Kreutz, James K. 109
Kuenhold, John 17, 75, 85–91, 95, 146, 169, 171
Kuner-Empson Company 60

L

Lang, Jack 116
La Raza Unida Party 70
Larson, Carl 60
Lasser, J.K. 38
Leahy, Patrick 134
Legal Aid and Defender program 73
Legal Aid Society 73
Legal Services Corporation (LSC) 131
Lewis, Betty 104
Lopez, John R. 109

Love, Governor John 107–110
LSC. *See* Legal Services Corporation (LSC)

M

Manzanares, Jesse 108–109, 114–115, 169, 171
Markey, Nancy 3, 11, 31–33, 136, 149
Martinez, Nato 53, 59
Martin Luther King 76, 111
Maryknoll Magazine 94, 172
McCarthy, Senator Joseph 39
Meeker Massacre 82
Miller, Dave 73
Miller, Don 118, 169, 171
Mobilization Youth Legal Services 85
Mora, Pvt. Dennis 122

N

Nagel, Robert "Bob" 126–129, 136, 169, 171
NARF. *See* Native American Rights Fund
Native American Rights Fund 79, 80
Nativity scene (crèche). *See* Denver City and County Nativity Scene
Nigeria 77
Nixon, President Richard 144
North American Finance and Investment Co. 134
Northwest Immigrant Rights Project 71

O

OEO. *See* Office of Economic Opportunity (OEO)
Office of Economic Opportunity (OEO) 9, 68, 71, 97, 109
Ortiz, Marianno 57
Otero, Ray 112

P

Peace Corps 53, 54, 65, 71, 76, 85

Pebeahsy, Frank 48, 52

Perez, Raymundo 'Tigre' 112–113

Peterson, Courtland H. 120, 125, 129

Petition for Rehearing and a Suggestion for Rehearing en Banc 123

Phantom Migrants, The 94

Pizzi, Bill 127, 129, 169, 171

Prakken, Bill 9, 13, 18, 40, 67–69, 73–75, 86, 97, 110, 111, 114, 117, 120, 131, 169, 171

R

Reagan, Ronald 130–131

Reese, Jerry 74

"Reggie" (recipient of Reginal Fellowship) 68, 86

Reginald Fellowship. *See* Reginald Heber Smith Community Lawyer Fellowship; *See also* "Reggie" (recipient of Reginal Fellowship)

Reginald Heber Smith Community Lawyer Fellowship 67, 68, 86

Retherford, Robert 150–151, 171

Rhodes, Deborah 130

Rice, Mr. J. L. 53–54

Richardson, Elliot L. 144

Roach, John 73

Rolling Stones, The 77

Rose-Avila, Magdaleno (Len) M. 32, 40, 69–73, 111–114, 117, 152–154, 169, 171

Rural Chamber of Commerce 107

Russell, Lord Bertrand 122

Russo, Rosemarie 143, 144

S

Salazar, Gregorio 100

Samas, Pvt. David 122

Sanchez, Jennie 97–99, 169, 171

Sanchez, Lionel 100

San Diego State [University] 70

Sandoval, Moises 94

San Luis Valley 81–85

Santa Clara University 130, 172

Sax, Joseph 86

Secretary of Agriculture 100–103, 156–157, 163

Seeger, Peter "Pete" 122

Sheldon, Karin 136, 142, 169, 171

Shriver, Sargent 9

Sinatra, Frank 77

Skip Chase Amendment 130

Smith, Reginald Heber 67, 86

Smith, Tommy 111

Smith, W. Reece 131

Snelling, Richard 134

Society of American Law Teachers (SALT) 119

Solomon Amendment 142

Southern Ute Tribal Court 150

South Royalton (So Ro) 132–133, 137, 150

state regulation 7 C.F.R. 862.15 100, 102

St. Gertrude Academy 74

Sugar Act 63, 166. *See also* Sugar Act of 1948

Sugar Act of 1948 101–103

Sunbeam 18–20

T

Taylor, Jennifer 56
Tenth Circuit 103
Teran, Ediberto 112

U

UCMJ. *See* Uniform Code of Military Justice
Umbrecht, Barbara 134–135
Uniform Code of Military Justice 122
United Farm Workers 105
United Farm Workers Union 164
United States Court of Appeals 17, 103, 123–124
University of Colorado rugby team 34
University of Michigan Law School 67, 85
University of Pennsylvania 67
University of Puget Sound Law School 38

V

Valdez, Jake R. 109
Valenzuela, Roberto 57, 58, 64
Vermont Law School (VLS) 132–154
Vermont Natural Resources Council 140
Vietnam War 38, 76, 77, 86, 122
VISTA 40, 61, 67, 75–76, 85, 94, 95
VLS Founder's Library 149
Volunteers in Service to America. *See* VISTA

W

War on Poverty 9, 67, 69, 76
Weld County General Hospital 15

Weld County Housing Authority 44, 53, 59

Weld County Migrant Council 57–58, 62

Wellman-Ally, Lisa 134

Western Resources Advocates 142

Williams College 27, 38, 68

Williams, Jack 107

Wirth, Senator Tim 148

Wittevrongel, Shelley 169

X

Ximenez, Vicente 63

Z

Zapf, Jim 169

For more information, to view online-only photos and to order additional copies of *Walkin the Walk While Talkin' the Law,* visit www.SkipChaseBook.com.

Stay in touch, share stories, and follow developments in social action, public interest and poverty law—
"Like" us on Facebook.

Made in the USA
Charleston, SC
07 January 2012